W9-CKQ-737

HELP,
I'm
Drowning

HELP, I'm Drowning

Weathering the Storms of Life with GRACE and HOPE

SALLY CLARKSON

BETHANYHOUSE
a division of Baker Publishing Group
Minneapolis, Minnesota

© 2021 by Sally Clarkson

Published by Bethany House Publishers
11400 Hampshire Avenue South
Bloomington, Minnesota 55438
www.bethanyhouse.com

Bethany House Publishers is a division of
Baker Publishing Group, Grand Rapids, Michigan

Printed in the United States of America

All rights reserved. No part of this publication may be reproduced, stored in a retrieval system, or transmitted in any form or by any means—for example, electronic, photocopy, recording—without the prior written permission of the publisher. The only exception is brief quotations in printed reviews.

Library of Congress Cataloging-in-Publication Data
Names: Clarkson, Sally, author.
Title: Help, I'm drowning : weathering the storms of life with grace and hope / Sally Clarkson.
Description: Minneapolis, Minnesota : Bethany House Publishers, [2021]
Identifiers: LCCN 2021015654 | ISBN 9780764235900 (cloth) | ISBN 9781493434633 (ebook)
Subjects: LCSH: Suffering—Religious aspects—Christianity. | Encouragement—Religious aspects—Christianity. | Faith.
Classification: LCC BV4909 .C567 2021 | DDC 248.8/6—dc23
LC record available at https://lccn.loc.gov/2021015654

Unless otherwise indicated, Scripture quotations are from the (NASB®) New American Standard Bible®, Copyright © 1960, 1971, 1977, 1995, 2020 by The Lockman Foundation. Used by permission. All rights reserved. www.lockman.org

Scripture quotations labeled ESV are from The Holy Bible, English Standard Version® (ESV®), copyright © 2001 by Crossway, a publishing ministry of Good News Publishers. Used by permission. All rights reserved. ESV Text Edition: 2016

Scripture quotations labeled NET are from the NET Bible®, copyright © 1996–2016 by Biblical Studies Press, L.L.C. http://netbible.com. Used by permission. All rights reserved.

Scripture quotations labeled NIV are from THE HOLY BIBLE, NEW INTERNATIONAL VERSION®, NIV® Copyright © 1973, 1978, 1984, 2011 by Biblica, Inc.® Used by permission. All rights reserved worldwide.

Scripture quotations labeled NKJV are from the New King James Version®. Copyright © 1982 by Thomas Nelson. Used by permission. All rights reserved.

Scripture quotations labeled NLT are from the Holy Bible, New Living Translation, copyright © 1996, 2004, 2015 by Tyndale House Foundation. Used by permission of Tyndale House Publishers, Inc., Carol Stream, Illinois 60188. All rights reserved.

Cover design by Patti Brinks, with Eric Walljasper

Author is represented by The Bindery.

21 22 23 24 25 26 27   7 6 5 4 3 2 1

Contents

Foreword

You're not alone.

If there is one truth, one piece of encouragement I could give you as you crack open these pages, it would be that whatever you are in the middle of, you are not alone. It's the truth I believed most of my life but found myself clinging to almost four years ago when my husband was diagnosed with incurable cancer. His diagnosis felt like a punch in the stomach. Every breath was a labor, a gasping for just enough air to fill my lungs. It all felt impossible.

How could I possibly survive? I would have to learn to walk through the unimaginable, and I have. Step by step we are moving forward. By the grace of God, my husband is alive today, and although he likely faces a lifetime of some type of treatment, we've experienced the goodness of God in our darkest moments. God has been with us all along.

I don't know what your storm is right now. Maybe it's a wayward child. Financial insecurity. An unfaithful spouse. Sickness. Or a miscarriage. But whatever it is, I am guessing you, too, have felt weary and wondered how you will get through what feels impossible.

Not long ago, I lay in bed thinking about someone just like you—the thousands of women who make up my online community. My heart felt tender toward all they may be facing. So right then and there I typed out a little prayer for the woman who was facing hard stuff in her life and hit *publish* on my Facebook page. In moments, hundreds of comments and shares were flooding in. Women pouring out their hearts desperately in need of prayer for the trials they faced. It's true. You're not alone. Women all over the world are searching for hope just like you. And the glorious truth is that not only is God forever by your side, but women all over the world are facing hard stuff as well.

There is just something about knowing that not only are you not alone because God is with you, but you are not alone because others have been there. We all need the friend whom we call out to in the middle of the storm. The friend who will walk with us through impossible circumstances and rescue us when we're drowning. In the pages of this book, Sally Clarkson is that friend. Over the years, she has been that dear friend to me, and her words have touched me countless times. With wisdom and love she will minister to your heart, point you to the true place for hope and peace, and yes, remind you that you are not alone.

Take courage, my friend. You will get through this. We will get through this. Together.

Ruth Schwenk, founder of TheBetterMom.com and coauthor
of *In a Boat in the Middle of a Lake: Trusting
the God Who Meets Us in Our Storm*

Letter to the Storm-Tossed

Precious One,

As you embark on your life journey with me, remember that I will be with you each step of the way. Nothing you encounter will be able to separate you from my love. Many life-storms will come across your path, but I am the One who calms the storms and provides you a way through the overwhelming darkness. I will light your way forward.

Storms will come in many forms. Snakes will crawl through your garden, tempting you to doubt my goodness. Fiery furnaces will manifest boldly to test your faith to the core. Lions will growl and threaten to overcome you with voices of despair. Giants will appear to fill you with fear and a sense of inadequacy to face the dangers looming ahead. Job's friends will boldly voice criticism and judgment to cause you to doubt your convictions and personal adequacy. You may even be shipwrecked by disasters and sudden squalls of worldwide dimensions. All of these storms are temporary. Don't give up, don't give in, even when your feelings suggest otherwise.

Understand that I will strengthen you; I will encourage you and remind you of my words to lead you on your path. Through your faith and faithfulness, I will build your character with each step, so that your soul will become beautiful and your spirit strong. If you walk holding my hand, listening to my voice, you will become a source of light and goodness to others along their pathway of life. And you will become a worthy guide to those who need your wisdom, friendship, and encouragement, those who long to know my love, too.

Not a day will be wasted. I will never leave you nor forsake you.

All my love,
Jesus

Introduction

He comforts us in all our troubles so that we can comfort others.

2 Corinthians 1:4 NLT

I am not afraid of storms, for I am learning how to sail my ship.

Louisa May Alcott

The summer azure-blue and white flower baskets I had hung, as I always did, were gently blowing in the mountain breezes of a new morning. My energetic, "love me, pet me, pay attention to me" beloved golden retriever, Darcy, was roaming over my yard as usual. Rocking in my familiar, squeaky chair on our front porch, tea in hand, generally gave me delight. But as I pondered the state of my soul, it seemed to be clouding over with darkness.

Spring *had* promised to be a total pleasure. I had even remarked to my husband, "What a great season. All of our kids seem to be faring well at this point in life, our ministry is as solid as ever, we are able to pay our bills, and we have so many opportunities to write and help people. This is a good and rare season! No drama at the moment."

Within a few days, everything I was looking forward to was canceled, suspended until further notice. My adult children's lives and finances were greatly affected by the sudden Covid-19 pandemic, and so much more instability was ahead. A long-anticipated visit to my son and his wife in New York City had to be canceled indefinitely. A visit from my oldest daughter, her husband, and my only two grandchildren was postponed because the country of England, where they live, had pretty much shut down. Five conferences where I hoped to speak were also scrapped. Stores, cafés, and favorite restaurants closed their doors, and all activities, including church, were suspended indefinitely. As I anticipated releasing a legacy book into the world, *Awaking Wonder*, every event we had planned, many podcasts, and all our hotel conferences were removed from my calendar. We ended up having to hire a lawyer to work on our behalf to avoid being liable for a great debt we would incur by canceling our conferences (which no one would be able to attend if we'd had them anyway).

As I pondered the state of my soul, it seemed to be clouding over with darkness.

Help, I'm Drowning!

During the first months of the lockdown of Covid-19, two friends' young adult children committed suicide. Daily, I received messages and letters from women whose husbands had left them or were acting violently or angrily toward their now-always-in-the-house children. Three friends had stage-four cancer, but I was unable to help or visit them. Two of my closest and oldest friends were isolated and battling serious depression and called me to ask for help and prayer. And all of my adult children were calling often, battling through the days of the pandemic alone and far from the comfort and security of home or familiar relationships.

Storms, disasters, violence, protests, and political division filled the news daily. Financial projections of doom loomed on the national horizon. I know that the stories of many all over the world were just as depleting, difficult, and challenging. We all bore the impact of disappointed expectations and an uncontrollable future.

As I sat by myself, again, pondering the previous twelve lonely weeks, when one had marched on much the same as another, I had the feeling that deep inside I was drowning, caught in the gale-force winds and waves of this dark season of my life.

On the outside, I was keeping up a good face, handling all the pressures and circumstances with as much calm as possible for the sake of those who were looking to me for stability. Yet, a feeling of helplessness and despair lay just below the surface; I felt out of control, like a victim caught in a continuous onslaught of unexpected storms without even a second to catch my breath or get my sea legs. Is it the way of every woman to keep everyone else above water as she slowly sinks under the weight?

Is it the way of every woman to keep everyone else above water as she slowly sinks under the weight?

It was at this point that I began to write this book. I could not have guessed that for more than a year, I would be locked down and waiting for the pandemic to be over. Weren't we all surprised by 2020 and 2021? What do we do when we have no idea how long it will be before our circumstances change? How do we face these storms that come unexpectedly and totally disrupt our lives? How can we find safety amidst the constant barrage of the turbulent winds and raging waves of the storms of life?

During the pandemic, I received literally hundreds of messages, notes, and emails from those who were discouraged, had a sense of being lost, and were fearful of what was ahead. Of course, we have *all* felt this way at various times. And from the vantage point of having finished over six decades of life, I have lived through many such seasons.

Storms Can Be Training Grounds

As a young woman who had just given my life to Christ, I told Him I wanted to serve Him and love Him, and that I would go anywhere and do anything He wanted me to do. Yet, year after year, my life was loaded with difficulties, challenges, conflicting relationships, and sadness. My temptation many times was to say, "Lord, is this how you treat your friends? I gave my life to you, and all I have had is trouble, year after year." Of course, I had an abundance of blessings as well. But for about twelve years in a row, it seemed one year was harder than the last.

As I look back now, I realize that those years were, in many ways, my training grounds for learning theology (the foundations of truth about God, His world, and our place in it) and of becoming a follower who could actually be about His work. Through my failures and struggles, I learned all about my own flaws as I saw the evil of the world, and I realized why we so desperately need God's salvation. Learning the hard lessons of the cost of love helped me see that I was a mere toddler when I first gave my allegiance to Him. He wanted me to strain toward maturity so that I really could be an agent of His hope, His love, and His truth in a world that so desperately needed it.

There is character built, humility learned, compassion developed, and sympathy kindled through the stormy parts of life. In some ways, I became a seasoned sailor through passages of darkness and emerged with hard-won wisdom, able to show others how to make it through.

I learned that life is not G-rated, and Scripture has never promised a squeaky-clean world. If I was to bring light and truth into a dark world as a follower of Christ, I would need to face the harsh realities of disappointment, despair, and difficulties in the real world with courage, faith, wisdom, and light given by Him and learned through the circumstances of my own life. People long for someone to identify with their temptations, failures, and scars as Jesus did, and to give them

> *I became a seasoned sailor through passages of darkness and emerged with hard-won wisdom.*

a way forward with compassion, redemption, and healing. We must enter into their reality in order to walk with them toward the light, toward the love and salvation of Christ.

And so my storms served a greater purpose for me in my walk with God and in my growth in understanding the nature of a fallen world better. I began to understand how to reflect the reality of His healing and loving presence into all of my circumstances and relationships, because of what He taught me. And then, seasoned from these experiences of learning from His Spirit through my journey, I could bring wisdom and sympathy for others through the challenges of their lives. God seems to always have a bigger purpose for those who follow Him. So it is with those willing to walk through storms with Him, ready to minister His grace to a fallen world.

The Reason for This Book

Jesus taught and trained His disciples so that when He left the earth, they would be able to give the same wisdom and comfort He had provided for them to others. God has been my faithful companion through all the seasons of my life. He promised, "I will never leave you nor forsake you." (Hebrews 13:5 ESV).

And He never has. As I look back, there were times when I *thought* He had left me alone, but as a child who has grown stronger under His training and guidance, in His presence, I can see that He has been with me through every circumstance of my life. God was my tutor in helping me to grow in wisdom and biblical understanding, stretching my character and spiritual muscle. I can see that His ways, when I clung to Him and chose to trust Him, were the very foundations upon which I could build a sustainable and secure life.

It has taken me a lifetime to learn the truth about what it means to suffer in this world and yet live to see the grace of God. I want to come alongside others so they will not feel as lost or alone as I often have.

I want you to know, my friends, that you are seen and loved in the place you find yourself right now. Our heavenly Father desires to comfort you and assure you of His presence and companionship, as well as His wisdom to show a way forward. Because during so many of these times in my own life I was alone and didn't have spiritual companions to lift me up or help me, I thought, *Maybe I can be of some comfort or help or be a compassionate counselor to others who, like me, have felt alone. I want to reach out so that others will not have to be miserable, feeling no one would understand them.* I want to help others know how to keep moving forward with real hope. We all need a fellow struggler who has gone before us through the storms of life.

> *We all need a fellow struggler who has gone before us through the storms of life.*

Most of all, I want you to know that right where you are today, in the middle of your story, you are seen. You are a treasure to God. He loves you so much more than you can imagine, and He is sorry for the pain you are feeling from being caught in the stranglehold of a broken, violent, rebellious world. There is a way forward to His grace that will help you find your way through. Every day you choose to walk with Him in faith you will be one day closer to finding true rest and peace in life as it comes. I hope you will find, from these stories of my many years of storms, that God deeply cares for you, He understands your feelings, He is present to comfort and sympathize, and He wants to give you hope to be able to come out of your own storms with grace.

I entered my adult life with such high ideals, with "rose-colored" glasses, especially as a young and new Christian. I wasn't aware of the battles ahead as a single adult, a young married woman, a mama through the years, a professional author/speaker, and now an older woman experiencing new challenges with my growing age. But through all the seasons, my wonderful God has proved to be faithful and wise in crying with me as I needed His sympathy, and giving me strength to make it through whatever storm had come my way.

I pray that this book will help give you a way to believe forward and encouragement and helps to keep taking one step at a time right where you are.

Don't Let the Darkness In

I wish I had understood earlier in my life that storms happen frequently to all people in every generation. I came to believe that often, "darkness is knocking at my door." But I also realized that I had a choice of how to respond to the darkness. I learned that I could exercise faith and self-control and say in my heart, "I will not let you in."

The key to resisting the temptation to allow darkness to control my life came from a conversation with a friend: *Observe without absorbing.* He and I talked about the principle of learning to observe circumstances and relationships in life, holding them at arm's length without absorbing the fear, threats of danger, or conflict into my heart. It is a habit, a way of facing storms without entering the stress of the consequences. This is, of course, a process that I had to practice over and over again. When one can stand solidly and fearlessly amidst the storms, there will be more stability, wisdom, and strength to live through the storm with perspective and wisdom.

Being Prepared for Storms Makes All the Difference

When I was a young mother, I learned the wisdom of having a first-aid illness-and-catastrophe box to meet the needs of my children. Bandages for skinned knees, decongestant for stuffy noses, asthma medicine for the bouts of breathing problems three of my children faced, and little remedies I had garnered through experience. This box of preparedness got me through many a rough circumstance of illnesses and scrapes.

Similarly, I discovered I needed to be prepared for the impending violence of the life-storms I had learned would always come my way. Over the years, I put together what could be termed a *storm-aid* box of some simple principles to go to, thoughts to give me a way forward, gathered wisdom, and remedies to help me find my sea legs during such times. These simple principles of "sailor readiness" became my go-to essentials to guide me through the challenges of life-storms. I kept them in the front of my personal journal so I could use them whenever darkness threatened to overwhelm. These tools provide calm and the ability to actually flourish amidst the devastating circumstances, to approach them prepared and with peace amidst the seeming chaos.

I found strength in foundational truths that I could hold on to.

Storms still bring me stress, and I still must battle through the rough seas. Yet, over the years, I found strength in foundational truths that I could hold on to for emotional and spiritual perspective, wisdom to bear up, and strength to endure. These are the "rock" Jesus spoke of when He said

19

to build our lives on the rock, so that when the storms of life come, our house does not fall (Matthew 7:24).

In this book I'll share with you these truths that have enabled me to sort out the ups and downs of my life and move forward. I will also address some specific storms: self-condemnation, a sense of failure, marriage stress, difficult children, demands and exhaustion in parenting, the inconsistencies of people in our lives, and other stresses that created havoc in my life.

Life Does Not Work by Formula

My answers are not prescriptive, one-size-fits-all, or formulaic. I won't tell you, "If you just believe these things or pray in *this* way, all will be well." Our stories are varied and differ greatly, and I know that some carry a heavy burden with devastating scars and deep anguish. But I have found that I need to sit with my Bible, to cry out in lament to Him, to seek the companionship of God, to wait for His answers, and to find His compassion, comfort, and wisdom to go forward. After my experiences over many years, I am better able to picture His nearness and truth, to allow Him to be God, and to absorb the truth that He does love me, that He is always faithful, that I am important to Him rather than invisible. And yet, I discovered that He was willing to bear with me in my doubts, my growing pains, my moving from toddlerhood to a more mature view of life. He was willing to be patient with me in the process.

To believe all of that becomes an offering of love from me to Him. I pray, "I thank you for the truth I know: that darkness is not dark to you, that you are here with me. Thank you for taking care of all these concerns and worries I have, though I have no idea how you are going to do so. Thank you for being faithful to me and helping me grow in faith. Thank you for holding me and protecting me, your toddler, while the storms of the world rage."

Through all the seasons, He was obviously doing so much more in my life than I could have known. He wanted to turn my direction and protect me from idolizing easy answers and quick fixes. He built godly character inside, even when I did not recognize it at the time. I experienced a closeness to Him from finding His fellowship in my sufferings and was able to understand Him more clearly. And I have been blessed by slowly learning to wait, to trust in His goodness, even when I could not see it. I have found a peace that cannot be shaken.

As a matter of fact, when I see where my children and Clay and I are, after all these years, when I observe God's faithful ways in my life and marriage, I often think He was doing far more than I had even asked Him to do. But even as a toddler doesn't understand the discipline, love, and protection of a wise parent, so in my limitations and ignorance, I was tempted to think He was not there, that He was not taking care of me.

We can be tempted to despair by the situations of life compounded by our own inner struggles and immaturity and lack of perspective. Many are falling into that endless cycle. Yet, I read this truth from God's Word in my quiet time today: "No one who hopes in you will ever be put to shame" (Psalm 25:3 NIV). My heart concurs because I have learned that it is true. He promises that when we wait on Him, praise Him, rest in Him, believe in Him, wrestle with Him, and cry out to Him, we will not be embarrassed of the faith we have placed in Him.

When these tests come upon us, they are moments when we are invited to look at our circumstances, acknowledge our feelings of despair, and evaluate the great waves that threaten to turn us adrift. In the face of it all, He enables us to choose to say by faith, "I don't understand, but I believe and I will wait, and I will rest, as an act of my will, because you are the Lord of Hosts and you are my Father. I am your beloved and trusting child."

I pray this book will be a light in your darkness. I pray it will be an encouragement and exhortation that enables you to rise above the threat of depression and difficulty, from the doom of despair and hopelessness. At the end of each chapter, this book will offer some anchors that you can lower and set to add stability to your life and the lives of those you love. By making decisions to intentionally set these moorings into our lives, we are enabled to combat the plan of the enemy to capsize our boat—and our faith.

I pray this book will be a light in your darkness.

May you and your own precious family reach safe harbor. I will see you there.

ONE

Does God Not Care?

We all feel dark sometimes

In this world you will have trouble. But take heart! I have overcome the world.

John 16:33 NIV

The fishermen know that the sea is dangerous and the storm terrible, but they have never found these dangers sufficient reason for remaining ashore.

Vincent van Gogh

I just don't think I can do this. I don't think I will make it through."

Have you ever felt like that? I have, many times. And yet, somehow, I am still alive and moving forward, one step at a time.

As I look back on the decades of my life, one thing I know is that storms are a natural part of life. Storms happen. Some seasons of life seem more storm-ridden than others. In nature, there are snowstorms, sandstorms, rainstorms, firestorms, tornadoes, hurricanes, and monsoons. In life, there are emotional storms, spiritual storms, physical storms, psychological storms, financial storms, marriage storms, child storms . . . you get the picture.

If I had been more prepared for the storms, they would not have surprised me and thrown me off my feet. To know the truth about something is to prepare to deal with the reality of that truth. I experienced so much anguish, doubt, fear, bitterness, and insecurity because I did not know life would be so hard, so often.

> *I experienced so much anguish, doubt, fear, bitterness, and insecurity because I did not know life would be so hard, so often.*

As I mentioned in the introduction, preparing for storms can help eliminate some of the emotional upheaval that comes when we are taken by surprise.

I would love to be able to say, "If you just follow these five steps, you will not experience the pressure, fear, or danger of storms in your life." I really wish I could take away the pain, horrible consequences, and unjust suffering I see in the lives of so many. Life is a sort of obstacle course. Yet, I can't pretend the problems away or find an instant solution.

There is no formula in this world to make suffering, injustice, evil, difficulty, and the consequences of living with immature and unloving people disappear. We all have unanswered questions like "Why did this terrible thing happen to me?" Even Jesus himself suffered a violent death at the hands of wicked people. Consequently, to give a flippant, prescribed answer to people's pain is not biblical.

So how do we move through the unanswerable, overwhelming darkness and pain common to all in life? How do we accept our own failures and learn to heal and move on?

We are usually all looking for quick fixes, and often, instead of waiting for God's answer or God's source of relief, we try in our own efforts to shorten the process by taking matters into our own hands. Sometimes we mess things up even further. We certainly do not want to stay in the middle of the storms of life and wait for them to be over. And yet, often, that is just what we have to do—wait them out.

As I began to pray about this book and to try to organize my thoughts, I realized that part of me really just wants everything to be okay. I avoid conflict like the plague. I would love to promise myself and my children that their lives will be without difficulty, conflict, or pain. If only I could protect them . . . But I can't control life, I can't make it behave, and I know from experience that there will continue to be storms in all of our lives. Until we deal with this reality, we will fight and rail against all challenges, relationship problems, and disappointed expectations, and feel we have lost our way.

As my children were growing up, I recognized that loving them well meant telling them about life's battles. I was not called to remove them from their own storms, or protect them from the stress, but to walk with them through the storms. Showing them how to be a faithful sailor is a gift that prepared them for their adult life. Teaching them these realities has allowed them to go into their worlds strong.

We see this struggle and surprise at the storm in the lives of the disciples when they found themselves in an unexpected tempest so violent they feared for their lives.

Difficulties Are a Natural, Normal Part of Life in the Broken World

> On that day, when evening came, He said to them, "Let's go over to the other side." After dismissing the crowd, they took Him along with them in the boat, just as He was; and other boats were with Him. And a fierce gale of wind developed, and the waves were breaking over the boat so much that the boat was already filling with water. And yet Jesus Himself was in the stern, asleep on the cushion; and they woke Him and said to Him, "Teacher, do You not care that we are perishing?" And He got up and rebuked the wind and said to the sea, "Hush, be still." And the wind died down and it became perfectly calm. And He said to them, "Why are you afraid? Do you still have no faith?" They became very much afraid and said to one another, "Who, then, is this, that even the wind and the sea obey Him?"
>
> Mark 4:35–41

The Sea of Galilee sits snug within the hills of northern Israel, a jewel of blue eight miles wide and twelve miles long, with its entire periphery visible from anywhere on shore. Its location, at 700 feet below sea level surrounded by mountainous terrain, makes it a prime spot for sudden, violent storms as powerful winds race down from the Golan Heights without warning. With depths reaching nearly 200 feet in an area often troubled by earthquakes, this is not a lake where storms can be treated lightly.

The disciples spent their day on the shores of this lake just as they had many times, surrounded by crowds of people pressing in to see and hear from Jesus. It was familiar to all of them, Simon and Andrew having fished here all their lives, and brothers James and John having been recruited into Jesus' band right here. Jesus had once again stepped into a boat and pushed out onto the water from these shores to tell them parables centered on the kingdom. By the end of the day, the men were all exhausted, grimy, and hungry, and probably longing for some quiet.

Now, as evening falls, they finally leave the people behind and step into a boat to travel to the other side, at Jesus' request. He himself is so exhausted He has fallen asleep on a cushion in the stern. As they sail across the lake, a storm suddenly arises. The clouds overhead gather and turn gray, then black; the water clouds, darkens, and begins to boil below them; the ship bobs on the water, listing from side to side; the wind whips the air around them into a powerful frenzy until the waves are driven over and eventually right into the little boat.

The men scramble in the pounding rain to keep afloat, grasping for blowing sails and soaking-wet rope, their oars useless, grabbing on to whatever they can hold and the sides of the boat, trying to save what little supplies they've brought along, while the storm lashes and tosses them until even the lifelong fishermen on board fear for their very lives. These men are used to storms; they are experienced sailors. But this terrible squall is different, worse, unexpectedly violent.

Finally, one of the disciples battles his way to the back of the boat, searching for Jesus. Surely surprised to find Him asleep, he desperately asks the question we, too, ask when we find ourselves tossed on a sea we cannot control, words pouring out like lament and accusation all in one: "Teacher, do you not care that we are perishing?"

It's confusing, isn't it? Here, right in the middle of Jesus' loving, teaching, encouraging, and training His disciples, He asks them to do something they've done multiple times before—cross the familiar lake where they have lived all of their lives. Yet before they reach the other side, right in the middle of doing what He had asked them to do, suddenly, their lives are in danger.

Right in the middle of doing what He had asked them to do, suddenly, their lives are in danger.

When I read this story, I wonder, and have verbalized their sentiment, too—*What could Jesus possibly be thinking? Does He want to lose all His disciples at once?*

Don't we ask these questions as well? *God, why are you allowing this to happen to me?*

Is He trying to discourage them? These men have given their whole lives to follow Him. Their hearts are dedicated to worshipping Him. They spend their days busily serving other people. And really, now this? Is this any way to treat those who are following you?

Ever have an inner narrative that sounded something like this? . . . *I am tired. I have worked to exhaustion. I have been faithful. I have cooked. I have washed dishes. I have lost years of sleep. I have loved and served and given—does anyone notice? I have been patient, forgiving. Does it matter? And now this?! Another storm? Another problem? Even more, what is happening to me is not fair. The relentlessness of life is about to drown me, Lord.*

Do you not care that I am perishing, Lord? This is the question we, like the disciples, have on our hearts.

Just when we have the ideals of our lives in place, when we have given our lives to Him, after we have determined to commit to make our home a place where the love of Christ will flourish, storms begin to overtake us, again, and we feel that we may be overcome.

The Presence of a Storm Doesn't Mean the Absence of God

Jesus did calm the storm. He commanded it to be still, and the waves, wind, and storm clouds obeyed him. He is the source of power over the storms. Yet He who knows all things did not prevent His disciples from being caught in the storm.

It is notable to me that when Jesus calms the storm, He does not say, "I'm so sorry you have been afraid and that this storm has caused you discomfort, bless your little hearts." Instead, He says, "*Why are you afraid?* Do you *still* have no faith?" (emphasis mine).

Jesus allowed this storm, and He was training His disciples to be able to handle storms.

It strikes me that Jesus—the perfect, compassionate servant-leader, all-knowing, all-loving—allowed this storm, and He was training His disciples to be able to handle storms. What does that say to me? It means that He wants me, like

His disciples, to face my storms with faith, believing that He is with me and capable of helping me, and will give me a way to survive. My part is to trust Him.

We can't make the storms cease or be tempered. We are in a world that is in rebellion against God, and Satan, knowing his time is short, is pouring out his wrath in this world (Revelation 12:12). *Wrath* is extreme hate and destructive anger.

The Bible teaches me that storms have been a part of life on earth from the beginning. Jesus spends a lot of verses informing His followers how to make it through them. Our loving God did not say He would make our lives easy and without pain, but He did say He would be with us and strengthen us and give wisdom so we could make it through the storms with His grace and hope.

Learning to live by God's provision and strength in His grace and developing hope that we will live to see and experience His ultimate love and blessing are the underlying themes of this book. God wants to companion us through our lives with wisdom so we can live deeply in His love even when life is falling apart.

Grace to Live a God-Dependent Life

Throughout Scripture God informs us of His grace—a force of strength and favor from God by which He carries us through our lives so we might be able to bear and flourish in all the circumstances that come our way. He told His disciples that He would leave His Spirit to encourage us, to strengthen us, to remind us of His words, to give us strength when we need it. The Spirit is the source of His grace.

But when He, the Spirit of truth, comes, He will guide you
into all the truth; for He will not speak on His own, but
whatever He hears, He will speak; and He will disclose to
you what is to come. He will glorify Me, for He will take
from Mine and will disclose it to you.

John 16:13–14

So many times in my life I have encountered the tension
between wanting to be filled with God's Spirit, strength,
wisdom, and graciousness, and then being overwhelmed by
my own attitudes, the unexpected situations of my life, or the
many clashing personalities of my family members. I often
fail to love and bring peace. Life tends to have a sandpaper effect on my attempts to be holy. Though I desire to be mature,
I get irritated at small issues. When I have a quiet time and
learn the wisdom of Scripture, I often then leave this place
and immediately disqualify myself by reacting wrongly to
the stress of my life or the person who created the calamity.
These times have led me to explore what it means to live
in the power of the Spirit, and to really exhibit the fruit of
the Spirit: "love, joy, peace, patience, kindness, goodness,
faithfulness, gentleness, self-control" (Galatians 5:22–23).

Throughout Scripture, the Holy Spirit is often described
using the analogy of wind or breath. When explaining the
mysteries of the Spirit to Nicodemus, Jesus said: "The wind
blows where it wishes, and you hear the sound of it, but you
do not know where it is coming from and where it is going;
so is everyone who has been born of the Spirit" (John 3:8).

The Greek word Jesus uses is *pnuema*, which can be translated as wind, breath, or spirit. Later, when Jesus is com-
missioning His disciples, Scripture manifests the metaphor

into an actual happenstance: "And when He had said this, He breathed on them and said to them, 'Receive the Holy Spirit'" (John 20:22).

Again and again the Holy Spirit is described as God-breath, which brings life, and wind, which provides direction. When we believe in Christ, His life breath enters our lives and we come to know Him as a real companion, and allow Him to slowly transform us to allow His breath to blow through our thoughts, our emotions, our actions.

Living in the power of the Spirit means letting Him be the breath that allows us to make it through every day.

Breath is a daily necessity; we cannot live without it. That same sort of dependence ought to be reflected in our reliance on the Holy Spirit. Living in the power of the Spirit means letting Him be the breath that allows us to make it through every day.

Christians Cannot Flourish without God's Spirit

To live only within the mundane constrictions of daily life is not to be alive at all. Christian means "Christ in one." When we live in Him, we are "in Christ Jesus." When I learned this secret—owning the Holy Spirit's strength in my life—I was transformed. I did not have to be perfect, I just had to walk with God, and trust Him, His Spirit, with my life. This is the way I have learned to bear the storms that come my way—knowing His presence living and breathing through me, His Spirit leading me step by step.

Christians cannot flourish apart from making God's Spirit the source of their spiritual lives. Even the phrase *spiritual life* refers to the Spirit-living-through-us life. This is not a strange, unique experience, but the fruit of God's Spirit living through our being, as described in Galatians 5:22–23: "The fruit of the Spirit is love, joy, peace, patience, kindness, goodness, faithfulness, gentleness, self-control." Living this way requires power we could never muster up on our own, but God's grace lives through us to show this fruit.

It might be described as:

- an inner strength
- a voice that calls us to become more excellent
- an energy that moves us to love and forgive supernaturally
- a fruitfulness that can only be explained by God.

When the Holy Spirit directs our course, the natural consequence is a life outside of normal striving and fleshly effort. We will find rest, comfort, and assurance that we are not carrying the weight of this world alone, but that He is within us carrying it and holding us through the storms. We are able to live beyond our own capacity with the grace God provides every day. The rest of this book will be looking at aspects of how this happens in a variety of storms that invade our lives.

We are able to live beyond our own capacity with the grace God provides every day.

Hope Leads Us Forward

One of the pleasures and deepest blessings of approaching my seventies is that I have come to understand my children were paying attention and noticing my own imperfect efforts to walk with God through my days. Now that they have had to endure so many difficulties and inequities in their own lives, their view backward has shown me my faith-walk mattered even more than I knew.

One day after a truly heartbreaking period of life for our family, one of my adult kids said to me, "Mama, one of the things that most distinguishes you is that you are always a hopeful person. No matter what happened, you always pointed us to hope, that God would redeem the circumstances of our lives in His time."

How surprised I was to hear this, as I have often felt that I was a struggler through the many challenges that threatened to overcome us.

Many years ago, I realized that children long to have a mostly happy, hopeful mother, because that is what it means to walk in the companionship of His Spirit. If we learn to trust God, we have hope. Our children are growing up in a time when media spread the gloom and doom of catastrophes, fears, and threats. When a mama spreads light and thankfulness and hope in the darkness, children feel secure and safe.

Children long to have a mostly happy, hopeful mother.

But when a mama lives darkly and complains about life, the children harbor fear and insecurity and sometimes blame themselves for their parent being angry or sad. Hope is not natural; it is supernatural. Hope comes welling up from deep inside because of a belief that God is good and He will win in the end.

Romans 15:13 is truly amazing: "Now may the God of hope fill you with all joy and peace in believing, so that you will abound in hope by the power of the Holy Spirit." The God of hope will fill us with (overflowing, endless, abundant) peace that we may abound in hope by the power of the Holy Spirit. There it is again—the hope and peace that come from the Holy Spirit's life through our own hearts and minds.

Hope is not a feeling; it is a commitment to hold fast to what Scripture reminds us is true about God. We must spend time with God, the Source of all that is good and wise and full of insight. The Word of God is the vocabulary of the Holy Spirit, giving us language so He may guide us as we need answers and wisdom to fight the storms well. Knowing Scripture, pondering it, and taking it into our souls, is what gives us fuel to live the Christian life. The only way to live well is to live in fellowship with God. Nothing else will satisfy.

Hope is an assurance that our King has ultimately won the raging battle.

We live in an imperfect world filled with disappointments, devastation, and difficulty. *Without hope, our lives can feel absolutely purposeless and powerless sometimes.* Circumstances will come our way, and we will always have a choice to make. We can choose to give up, or we can choose *hope.*

Hope is an assurance that our King has ultimately won the raging battle. Hope teaches us that this is the broken place yet here we have the honor of believing Him who is fighting on our behalf.

Hope Anchors the Soul and Keeps Us Grounded

> This hope we have as an anchor of the soul, a hope both sure and reliable and one which enters within the veil.
>
> Hebrews 6:19

When we have nothing else to rely on, our hope in God is what connects us to what is true. As Romans 15:13 tells us, when we put our trust in God, we can *overflow* with hope. This hope from the Holy Spirit is such a powerful entity it can make us truly unstoppable.

But faith is a choice that requires us to relinquish our fears, doubts, and worries into the hands of God, like a child who says, "I will trust my mama and daddy because I know they are good and loving and reliable." So we say, "I will give this into His hands because I know He is good and loving and reliable."

Hope Gives Us the Strength to Take On Our Future

Hope can cure the incurable heart. No circumstance, no problem, no issue, no devastation is too large or too difficult for God to take on. However, we have to choose this hope as a part of our worship of God. We hope for an eternal life with Him where His kingdom will have no end. We focus not on what is seen, but on the place He is taking us, to a wedding feast He has prepared for us, His bride. We must learn to believe and accept this hope. Sometimes, life can beat us down and make us feel absolutely defeated. But when we choose to carry the hope God has given us, we are able to overcome anything.

> Now faith is the certainty of things hoped for, a proof of things not seen.
>
> Hebrews 11:1

My hope rests in God's character and ability to see me through. He answers prayer. He is always good. He has overcome the world. He has forgiven every sin. He will never leave me or forsake me. I can leave my issues in the file drawer of heaven and know that He has the ability to work them out and to cause "all things to work together for good to those who love God" (Romans 8:28).

The God-given gift of hope is the best possible medicine for any hardship in life. My hope says I am willing to wait on God's timing, God's way, and God's will with a belief that I will look back and be amazed at the ways He showed His faithfulness. My hope is what carried me through health issues, struggles in my family, going five years without a salary, and so much more. Hope is the physician of each misery, and God has given us this gift to heal us from our pasts so we may have a future that is full of joy and light.

The God-given gift of hope is the best possible medicine for any hardship in life.

Yet, we are babies moving from immaturity toward maturity. Learning the grace of walking in the Spirit, as mere toddlers learning slowly, allowing God to hold us through the storms, is a process of growth. Even as my children had to learn to trust me, to obey my requests, to trust my wisdom, so our walk toward maturity in Christ is a process. I hope the chapters ahead, where I share my own experience in many different storms of life, will be of encouragement to you as you face your own storms.

An Anchoring
PRAYER

Precious Heavenly Father,

Sometimes I wonder if I am invisible. Do you know how much I struggle? Do you see me in my storm? Yet I know your Word tells me you love me, that you are always with me, somehow. I humbly acknowledge that you are faithful and that you see me and know my battles. Lord, I want to choose to be a person of hope because of my faith in you. Please take my burdens into your own hands, and through the Holy Spirit, restore my heart to peace. Let my choice to praise you please you, because my spiritual service of worship is to hope in you each day. Thank you for your patience and love for me. I love you, too, sweet Lord.

I come to you in Jesus' name. Amen.

An Anchoring
SCRIPTURE

Do not be anxious about anything, but in everything by prayer and pleading with thanksgiving let your requests be made known to God. And the peace of God, which surpasses all comprehension, will guard your hearts and minds in Christ Jesus.

PHILIPPIANS 4:6–7

Whenever I am feeling stressed or anxious, the Holy Spirit brings Philippians 4:6–7 to mind. "Do not be anxious about anything," it implores. Does this seem like an impossible demand? What clue does the rest of the verse give us about how such a way of life might be possible?

Considering this and the verses from this chapter, what is the value of hope? Where does it come from? Are you walking in hope now?

An Anchoring
ACT

When my feelings dip (and sometimes crash!), I find it helps me to copy the writers of the Psalms: I sit down with a notebook and pen and write down what's in my heart. I let all my anxieties and worries and cares spill out onto the page. Sometimes it's in the form of a list, sometimes something a bit more like a letter. While I begin with the hard and negative parts, my words eventually come around, which helps my feelings come around to a brighter place along with them. Try writing your own psalm this week during your devotional time.

TWO

We're in Good Company

Lament is legitimate; it's okay to be sad

No temptation has overtaken you except something common to mankind; and God is faithful, so He will not allow you to be tempted beyond what you are able, but with the temptation will provide the way of escape also, so that you will be able to endure it.

1 Corinthians 10:13

There are some things you learn best in calm, and some in storm.

Willa Cather

Recently, I was looking back at journals and could see a trail, my pathway of life through years of memories recorded there. Looking through the pages, I was struck by how I had seen the love and goodness of God through the years, even when I could not at the moment feel it. Mostly, I found the ability to see His grace in many difficult times *only after waiting long enough* to allow Him to resolve each battle, each struggle, each question. I wish I had understood then that, from the beginning of the world until the end, purposeful living will always exact a cost, that the work of life is often tedious and demanding, that there are battles to be fought in small and insignificant places where faithfulness is required. I know now I can find hope because God desires to companion me every single day in the weary times as well as when we celebrate. Through His Spirit, He has given us capacity to live into strength for the journey we will walk.

How well I remember one season as though it were happening today. It was a time when I was learning the ways of soldiering faithfully and finding that every day of choosing to be faithful was profoundly important to the overall legacy I would leave as "my story."

Midway through the years my children would live at home, I was the mother of children spanning from teens to a toddler. We had recently moved for the eighth time. Sarah, thirteen, was a budding teen with all the hormones and feelings. Joel, eleven, still loved his Legos and was delighting in being part of a performing boys' choir. Nathan was almost nine and bursting with energy, voice, opinions, and creativity. Joy, at almost three, was puttering everywhere in the house, exercising her extroverted personality, and having difficulty breathing every night around one in the morning. Clay was working away from home five nights a week, and I was premenopausal in my mid-forties and dealing with my own raging hormones.

One evening the sun was setting, and as the darkness overtook my bedroom, it seemed to overtake me as well. I actually wanted to stay in the darkness and hoped no one would find me. While daylight left the corners of the room, my heart felt as if it could melt into the same darkness, my mind feeling muddled and my feelings a blur.

Was there any way to escape? I wished to be invisible.

But no. My life wouldn't allow me to disappear, and even if I did, my thoughts would come along. I wondered at God's choice of me as a mother. Why had He given me these children, whom I loved so much yet felt so overwhelmed by sometimes? Perhaps, as one of my "Job's friends" said, He wanted me to feel like an abject failure to humble me? That was just how I felt: incapable of keeping up with the laundry, the dishes, the messy pantry; unable to manage things in the orderly way I wished and believed necessary.

> *As the darkness overtook my bedroom, it seemed to overtake me as well.*

Storm upon Storm

On top of it all, here I was with a ministry to thousands of moms. A recent encounter had thrown another bit of pain and confusion into my mind. A young couple we had mentored and taken under our wings had said they wanted to treat us to dinner. As they lived out of town, we had to plan our time ahead when they would be traveling to our city. How excited we were to think someone would care for us, as it was usually us reaching out and caring for everyone else! As the chosen night approached, Clay and I talked about how nice it would be to have a carefree evening, where we could relax and not be in charge of anything but just enjoy a meal with friends. The evening did not go as we expected, however. Soon after we began eating, our friends began confronting us about the wrong motives they supposedly saw in our hearts. They accused us of trying to take over other ministries and of actions we had never ever been involved in and words we had never uttered. They ended up literally yelling at us in the restaurant!

The truth was that Clay and I had gone without a salary for almost five years, just trying to be faithful to reach out to parents. Our first conference had eleven people. Our lives had required lots and lots of faith and long-suffering as we kept building messages and reaching out to parents in need of encouragement and training. We were shocked by the loud emotional blows that left deep bruises and wounds in our hearts and minds. This attack took us totally by surprise.

Naturally, these unexpected and unjustified accusations from fellow believers had left me a bit fragile of heart. My defenses down, I allowed a floodgate of thoughts to attack my vulnerable places with accusing and condemning words. How could I go on telling women how to disciple and encourage and inspire their children when I had been so sad and had neglected all of our own routines lately with my children? Coping with the demands of everyday life was all I could do the last few weeks. Why wasn't I more patient, less frustrated with messes and arguing and whining and boy noises? Why did my sweet children, whom I loved, drive me crazy, if God meant for me to be a mama?

It was a perfect soul storm that almost caused me to crater. I was looking for someone to blame. My children, of course, were the direct result of having gotten married long ago, so maybe the problem actually began much earlier: *Perhaps I should never have gotten married*, I thought. *Responsibilities for people are just too overwhelming, and I'm not much help to Clay, anyway.* You can see how I was spiraling down.

Because Clay was out of town from Sunday night through Thursday every week, I felt I deserved extra credit for caring for all of my children alone. As the clock ticked on, I realized that the pressures of the past several months were just too much, making me feel like the walls were closing in around me. My house felt more a prison than a haven at this moment, and I longed for escape.

> *It was a perfect soul storm that almost caused me to crater.*

I understand now that the havoc of my own life is often what other women in my life are experiencing. They need to know they are not the only ones moving through such dark and demanding days, and they need hope that somehow going forward one step at a time really does matter.

Escape wasn't to be found, of course. So, I pulled myself up again by sheer will and endeavored to engage in the usual tasks of late evening, letting the children know no challenges over bedtime routines would be tolerated, warning them this wasn't the night to get out of bed for water—or for any other reason! Thankfully, they cooperated, and I was able to eventually collapse into bed, grateful for the darkness that helped me fall asleep almost immediately.

Moving from Darkness to Light

The next morning's sunlight was unable to dispel the darkness that still enveloped me. Making my way to the kitchen, I was surprised to find myself still carrying the weight of it, the exhaustion palpable, like something I was dragging in my wake. Pouring a cup of tea and making my way to the couch in the living room for my usual morning quiet time, I found my soul dry and sluggish, too. The children woke and joined me one at a time on the surrounding couches and chairs, their questioning eyes reflecting my dullness. The room felt heavy, uncharacteristically quiet. I realized I needed to relieve the anxiety they were feeling, as I knew they weren't responsible for my feelings.

"Okay, everyone! I need your help today. There are several things that need to be done, and I cannot do every task myself. Can you pitch in?" They nodded as if responding out of insecurity or fear at their mama's sad face, and I assigned each a household or childcare duty in turn. I realized outer order wouldn't be able to fix all the deep wounds I was dealing with, but nevertheless it made me feel a bit more in control to at least have a plan and some help. The kids headed into their tasks with unusual determination, serious about each detail, and I joined them in my own duties in a more half-hearted manner.

Unfortunately, my emotions were still dampened as the day went on, and the next day as well. And I wasn't the only one affected; I could see the children's moods lowering right along with my own.

Finally, I had an idea: a special evening with a favorite novel we had been reading together and mugs of hot chocolate and popcorn around the fireplace. They agreed enthusiastically, and everyone scattered to do their part to make this vision take shape.

Suddenly, I heard Nathan's voice over all the excitement. With every bit of exuberant, boyish energy he possessed, he announced, "We are the very best family in the whole world! I feel sorry for everyone else who doesn't have all the fun we do!"

His proclamation stopped me in my tracks. How funny! Here I was, feeling like I wanted to crawl under a rock, and my precious little boy was just bubbling over with happy life. My eyes swept the room and took in my sweet Sarah, lovely, quiet, and thoughtful; Joel, my always sympathetic and loving renaissance man; and darling Joy, ever ready to crawl into my lap and pat me and kiss my cheek. I was suddenly overwhelmed by gratitude for these wonderful blessings God had given me. I was reminded how blessed I was just to have them in my life, as each was truly so precious and irreplaceable to me. As I took in the crackling fire and homey mugs and the dog on the hearth, I was grateful for the home life we shared together.

I had wondered two days before how I could go on in my tiring yet sometimes mundane life with them, and now I realized I couldn't live without them!

When evening came and I once again retired and thought over my day from under the covers, I was shocked at how my emotions had swung from darkness to light that day. The thoughts began again, but this time with a little humor thrown in . . . *Do I have some kind of disorder happening? Am I schizophrenic? What on earth is wrong with me? Maybe I am just not very spiritual. How is it possible to feel so down one day and then so grateful and content the next—when nothing has changed? How dare I feel depressed when I have such a good life! Am I just incredibly immature? Does anyone else ever experience mood swings like this, or am I the only one? How could I have made life so miserable for my precious ones the past few days? How could I have had such negative thoughts about my life and everyone in it?*

Have you ever had thought-swings like mine? I hadn't yet learned that my struggles were normal and that it was okay for me to feel such a sense of lament over my life. As I wrestled, I also sensed God's presence with me, and the guilt slowly abated. Remembering that negative thoughts and feelings and days are just a normal part of a busy woman's life helped me relax. I recalled that in many places, the psalmists expressed even darker thoughts than those I had been having, even as they worshipped God with their words.

Some darkness is warranted and some lament is justified.

Looking back now, I have gained perspective. I am a normal human being with emotional, physical, spiritual, and soul needs. All human beings have limits. My personality becomes more sensitive and introspective when I am exhausted, and the feelings I have at those times are not totally objective. When I feel dark, often I just need to peer into my heart and mind and take account of my health and well-being. Often a time to sleep, eat, and refresh with people and activities that give me vitality will enable me to move into a better place. I have also learned that some darkness is warranted and some lament is justified, and there is no reason to feel guilty when that is the case.

When I Lament, I'm in Good Company

People throughout Scripture experienced doubts, discouragement, and the feeling that they were alone. Complaints, sadness, anger, bitterness, and accusations are all a part of the laments found in the Psalms. This book is a record of the countless feelings people felt deeply and expressed honestly and wholeheartedly to God in prayer.

Complaints, sadness, anger, bitterness, and accusations are all a part of the laments found in the Psalms.

Many other passages and stories also tell of the difficult circumstances and accompanying feelings in the lives of others who walked with God over centuries. Paul speaks of this in his letter to the Corinthians, writing:

> For even when we came into Macedonia our flesh had no rest, but we were afflicted on every side: conflicts on the outside, fears inside. But God, who comforts the discouraged, comforted us by the arrival of Titus; and not only by his arrival, but also by the comfort with which he was comforted among you, as he reported to us your longing, your mourning, your zeal for me; so that I rejoiced even more.
>
> 2 Corinthians 7:5–7

We had no rest . . . we were afflicted . . . conflicts without, fears within . . . depressed . . . longing, mourning. . . . Amazing words from a man who Jesus called to serve His people in leadership! I actually have to admit that when I read the passage by Paul in 2 Corinthians about his feelings of depression, it made me feel better about myself! After all, if Paul, the great hero of the faith, had been depressed, then maybe there was hope for me! I discovered it is not a sin to be discouraged or depressed, but our response to those feelings is what determines our long-term well-being or lack thereof.

In times of difficulty and disappointment, it is evidently normal to be tempted to withdraw from God. Often, we take our negative feelings and stuff them down, assuming they are too ugly for Him to look at. We assume He would be angry with our unhappy reactions to life's circumstances. The Bible confronts that fear, though. In this Book we find so many others sharing their feelings with the Lord—from the dark side of the spectrum of emotion to the bright side. God, in His mercy, included countless stories of those who were discouraged, doubting, and lonely to help us know that He understands, that this is a normal reaction to life in a fallen, rebellious world. As I mentioned in the last chapter, more than two-thirds of the Psalms are full of lament as the author pours out prayers amid difficulty and trial.

Have you ever felt you needed to hide your feelings from the Lord? Have you ever felt He would be disappointed in you if you were discouraged, or even if you had doubts or complaints? He is not surprised, nor does He condemn you.

A lament is simply a complaint, a moaning or groaning in reaction to perceived injustice or difficult situations. I am so encouraged that these writers felt free to express their grief over not being able to see or feel God at times along their own paths.

We also find encouragement in the book of Hebrews, as new believers are exhorted to stay strong and reminded of all who have gone before them, strengthening them as they begin to weary in their walks with God under persecution. Jeremiah holds songs of sorrow over the sins of God's people, as the discipline that falls on them shows the depth of their needs. John's gospel reminds me that among Jesus' final words to His beloved disciples was this combined warning and encouragement: "In the world you have tribulation, but take courage; I have overcome the world" (16:33). The Spirit uses a reminder of this Scripture so often to bring grace to my hard days.

God Sympathizes with Us through All of Our Struggles

One of the weights I have carried through the years is this misunderstanding that somehow God is disappointed with me when my faith is less than perfect. I know there is nothing I can do to deserve the love and grace of God, but somehow it is written on my heart because of years of bad theology that He is looking for my performance, not my heart.

The writer of Hebrews knew that those he was writing to were discouraged. He knew they needed to see what God was really like, and we need to see this reality, too. In referring to Jesus as our intercessor who prays for us day and night, Hebrews 4:15–16 tells us:

> For we do not have a high priest who cannot sympathize with our weaknesses, but One who has been tempted in all things just as we are, yet without sin. Therefore let's approach the

throne of grace with confidence, so that we may receive mercy and find grace for help at the time of our need.

Jesus lived, walked, ate, and slept on this very earth where we live. He experienced broken relationships, pain and suffering, temptation, disappointment, and death. He was a human being who felt deep need and weariness and all the emotions of life we feel. He can sympathize with our weakness, and He understands our fragility. He was tempted, too.

I actually picture it like this: While we are struggling, Jesus is sitting near—perhaps with His arm around us—praying for us, cheering us on that we might make it through our darkness with faith intact. We are told in this passage that we can approach the throne of grace—not the throne of condemnation, but the throne of *grace*, where He is ready to listen and help, so that we might receive mercy and grace in our time of need. It is quite amazing to realize that in every situation, in every moment of our lives, Jesus is there as our defender, our advocate, our God, ready to comfort us with sympathy and understanding.

While we are struggling, Jesus is sitting near.

One of my favorite passages in Scripture underlines His sympathetic heart. Jesus is in the midst of a life of ministry to thousands of people who surrounded Him each day. We know that they were like all of us, some hurting, some prideful, some confused, some idolatrous, some selfish—just like the crowds of people surrounding us. As God, He could see their hearts. Yet we are told that "Jesus was going through all the cities and villages, teaching in their synagogues and proclaiming the gospel of the kingdom, and healing every disease and every sickness" (Matthew 9:35). And then in the next verse Matthew reminds us: "Seeing the crowds, He felt compassion for them, because they were distressed and downcast, like sheep without a shepherd" (v. 36).

The reaction of Christ to our needs, feelings, and struggles is to see us and have compassion on us. As our Good Shepherd, He wants to care for us, to tend to our needs, to protect us, to lead us to still waters, and to restore our souls.

God knows our fragile human state. It is why He gave His life for us. He looks at us with gentle, generous love just as a loving parent looks at his own precious child who is suffering. If we *really* lived into this reality, if we came to Him with all of our thoughts and feelings as one does to an intimate, trusted companion, we would find the grace of His sympathy and the hope of His help.

We Need to Depend on the Word of God

Throughout the difficult seasons of my own life, the Word of God has become my stronghold—my comfort and anchor to keep me going forward one step at a time. I have examined its words until they are etched on my heart, reading the Psalms more times than I can count. These words and stories have comforted, encouraged, and hidden me as I underlined and recited them to myself over and over again.

There were so many throughout the history of scriptural times who could identify with us. David was very clear about his own dark times. Sarah spent the vast majority of her life childless and then was subverted by the handmaiden she gave to her husband. Jeremiah had such a life that he is called the weeping prophet. Job suffered nearly incomprehensible calamity. Then there are the stories of Naomi and Jonah and so many more. Through God's Word we learn that in the darkness of our own lives, we are not alone. Not only are we not alone—we are surrounded in a way by other women and men who have walked with God and yet suffered deep, sometimes paralyzing, grief, confusion, and despair.

Through God's Word we learn that in the darkness of our own lives, we are not alone.

Seasons of darkness, weariness, discouragement, and exhaustion will come, and we are companioned. Not only do we have countless others whose stories validate our own challenges, but Jesus himself is literally present with us at every moment. He will give us the grace we need to walk through our journey. He will also grant us the hope that He gives us a way forward as He did with all of His children throughout biblical history. My friend, you are not alone; you have an Advocate, a Shepherd, a heavenly Father who wants to companion you through all your life.

An Anchoring
PRAYER

Dearest Lord,

My feelings feel so large sometimes, as if they could carry me away. I get angry, or feel depressed, or frustrated; then I feel guilty because it seems like I shouldn't feel this way. When I have time with people I can trust, though, I find I'm not the only one. Even in the absence of whispered secrets, I read the true confessions of your people in the Bible, and know those who live closely with you still find themselves struggling sometimes. Lord, remind me that you know I'm only human and you are a loving parent to me. I am so grateful for that truth! Oh, God, let me allow your love to encompass me as you lead me to still waters. In Jesus' name, Amen.

An Anchoring
SCRIPTURE

To You, LORD, I lift up my soul.
My God, in You I trust,
Do not let me be ashamed; . . .
Guard my soul and save me;
Do not let me be ashamed, for I take refuge in You.

> Let integrity and uprightness protect me,
> For I wait for You.
> Redeem Israel, God,
> From all his distress.

PSALM 25:1–2, 20–22

God longs to hear the cry of your heart. And when there are no words, reading the Psalms is a beautiful way to get some of those cries out.

Shame is an extremely powerful emotion. Have you ever felt yourself feeling ashamed over something you've done, or perhaps what looks like God's abandonment of you? Isn't it good to know you are not alone, even in this?

What might it look like for you to wait on God in this situation? Can you think of ways your integrity and uprightness might preserve you?

An Anchoring
ACT

Make a list of Bible characters you know who have faced difficulties and what their reactions were.

Do you know any people personally who seem godly and undeserving of trouble, yet you know they have some? Add them to the list. Write "I am in good company" at the top and put this list somewhere you can pull it out when you need the reminder.

THREE

Loneliness and Isolation

Finding hope when you feel all alone

And let us consider how to stir up one another to love and good works, not neglecting to meet together, as is the habit of some, but encouraging one another, and all the more as you see the Day drawing near.

Hebrews 10:24–25 ESV

We know the race is not to the swift nor the battle to the strong. Do you not think an angel rides in the whirlwind and directs this storm?

John Page

As I arrived at my door with two very full, heavy bags of groceries in hand, I fiddled with my keys, finally putting the bags down so I could open the front door. As I leaned down I was surprised to see sitting there the loveliest bunch of burgundy roses with baby's breath intermingled. Somehow, I had not noticed this delightful gift over my bags. A card was attached to the bundle. I took a moment to open it and read, wondering who could have possibly left such a beautiful gift on this, a normal, mundane sort of day.

I opened and read.

> Sally, I love you. I am grateful you are my sister-friend. I never had a good mama, or a sister to share life with, but God knew I needed kindness, sympathy, and compassion, and so He brought you into my life. I will always be there for you and know you will be there for me. Friends, forever.

Sudden tears flowed down my cheeks. I didn't even know they were near the surface, ready to flow, but this unexpected thoughtfulness with such precious words hit a tender place in my heart.

I am so used to "braving up" and stuffing my own needs that often I am not even aware that I long for companionship and a friend to walk beside me. Sometimes living courageously is our only option as life often leaves us desolate, without the companionship of kindred spirits.

The Pain of Loneliness

Sometimes the pain of loneliness is visceral, so it almost feels like a physical pain. It has been a companion of mine most of my life. Because I was a preemie baby and born at just thirty-one weeks, I was left at the hospital in a baby oxygen tent for two months without my mama. She said that because I was not quite three pounds, she was afraid to hold me when she visited the hospital. She thought I might break.

Bonding with children was not quite a well-accepted concept yet, so I stayed in the hospital being cared for by differing staff off and on for two months. I am sure they probably talked to me and must have touched me, and surely someone held me from time to time. But my children have said, "Mama, that story must explain why you always have this deep-seated feeling of loneliness."

Could it also be that Clay and I have moved nineteen times, which meant having to start over with friends, again and again? New to groups, new to churches, new to neighborhoods, new doctors, new everything. Or could it be that since my personality according to Myers-Briggs is that of only one percent of Americans, I feel different and a little out of the norm because in reality I am?! Perhaps it was because we have spent most of our lives isolated, away from family on holidays, birthdays, and major events.

Not all women feel this deep sense of isolation and loneliness, but many do. It is a storm that slowly builds and then comes crashing in when we are finally aware that we were never created to bear the burdens of life alone.

Longing for a Kindred Spirit

Flying somewhere between Dallas and Colorado, I had just finished speaking at a conference with nine hundred women. Many stood in line for two hours at the end of the day just to meet me and have me sign a book. The funny thing is that though so many people had traveled and made a lot of effort to sit and listen to me and then meet me for just a moment, I still left feeling isolated and lonely.

Always, though I loved the work and ministry I had been a part of for so many years, I would leave conference weekends ready to escape the crowds to creep into a place of rest and hiding, escaping to the comfort of my own place.

As I looked out over the dark clouds during the early evening flight, I felt there was a storm brewing inside. Deep, dark loneliness was a constant companion of my heart for many years. I ached inside for a friend, or someone who cared for me—someone who would notice me *personally*—not for what I could bring to them, give them, or do for them, but someone who cared for me as Sally Clarkson, human being, friend. As a relationship-oriented person, I had known deep friendship during much of my younger life, but it seemed that once I became an adult, a busy mother, a writer, a ministry leader, a speaker, and an idealist, it was more difficult to find anyone who was there for me personally—and rarely did someone reach out to me personally.

Deep, dark loneliness was a constant companion of my heart for many years.

Pouring out for three days to hundreds of women had used all my adrenaline. It took me years to realize that often, when I had spent myself, negative thoughts were a part of the emptiness that followed a big event. Honestly, I did have people who loved me and friends in many different parts of the country, even all over the world. But as an introvert (at least after conferences) I longed for someone who could understand my inner feelings and thoughts, the very ones that brought people to my writing and speaking.

It's funny to many, but it wasn't some kind of adulation or popularity that I wanted. I had learned years before that those things never satisfied my inner longings. But I longed for someone in my personal space who shared the commonplace moments of life: the stresses, struggles, joys and pleasures, and ideals. My inner-circle friends were often hundreds or thousands of miles away and so, often, I would quietly enter my home with a suitcase of clothes needing to be washed, messes of mail, and the evidence of having rushed out of the house to catch a plane all around. When finally home, I wanted to process all that had happened with someone close, to have a long walk together, to drink a cup of tea and talk on my porch for hours about our longings, feelings, struggles, hopes, and dreams. Just a comfortable friend who understood the complexities of my personality, family, and life demands.

I wasn't the only one in our family feeling this way. Clay and I struggled with this as a couple. Even my children longed for the "kindred spirits" Anne of Green Gables spoke of—people whose hearts are carved the same ways ours are carved. The illusion was that if we moved to a new town or joined a new church or group, we would find people like us with whom to share deep friendship.

We faithfully attended many groups, meetings, studies, and activities, but found we were mainly the ones reaching out, hosting the dinners, seasonal celebrations, and fun events. People always filled our home and responded to our invitations, but it was rare for us to be invited back.

I remember once when Sarah was washing dishes after a gathering at our home, again, and said, "Wouldn't it be nice if sometime someone would invite our whole family over for dinner and we wouldn't have to be the ones who cooked, cleaned, and washed dishes?"

Even as a twelve-year-old, she wondered at the seeming loneliness of our family as a group. The kids often made friends over the years as we would move from place to place. And we always had people we hung out with, but very few kindred spirits. God had made our family exceedingly idealistic, artistic, verbal, and very close-knit. Our family felt close to each other, but it was often hard to find a match with another.

A sense of isolation exploded during the Covid-19 pandemic. The diverse response to politics and cultural issues increased the sense of being alone for many, and finding someone who shared ideals was an even more elusive practice.

Ernest Hemingway, another idealistic writer, expressed it this way:

> The best people possess a feeling for beauty, the courage to take risks, the discipline to tell the truth, the capacity for sacrifice. Ironically, their virtues make them vulnerable; they are often wounded, sometimes destroyed.

These familiar thoughts filled my mind as we flew through the cloudy night. Tears gathered and spilled over as I wondered if I would ever feel complete, understood in this area of longing. This was a storm that raged over and over again, like seasonal blizzards that always leave devastation in their wake.

The Devastation of Isolation

The longing for friends, community, and belonging are legitimate feelings which, in a perfect world, God wanted to be fulfilled. The absence of a community of people where we belong and feel accepted and loved can create great anxiety and depression.

I did find other stalwart, exceptional friends who became very dear through years of growing together and living through so many seasons of life, but it took a long time to find those deeply satisfying friendships and then to build into them in all seasons over many experiences. We are more precious to one another for the isolation we each felt in our own living places during 2020.

In the midst of the isolation of the pandemic, with my children far from home, I was reminded of my previous feelings. Memories from the past flooded my mind as I sat on our Colorado deck one summer evening. The little fire pit crackled with flames as mountain breezes flitted through the space, mirroring the thoughts dancing through my mind. This time, though, I was thinking about the vacuum so many precious ones in my life had been feeling, without the hope of an answer.

During those months of isolation, these are some messages I received:

- I am so lonely and feel so exhausted from the 24/7 care of my family with no way to escape.
- I love my children, but it seems like I can't control my anger and frustration with them. I feel guilty all the time for losing my temper.

- My husband has gone into a deep depression, having to stay home and being surrounded constantly by children with the worries that we won't be able to pay our bills.
- I deeply miss my friends, our church, and groups where my children and I used to gather.
- I just wish I had support systems so I could actually have time to regroup.
- My mother (others said mother-in-law) does not understand my values and criticizes me all the time.
- My friends and I have different opinions about politics and issues being covered every day in the news. They do not understand me, and I can't believe they have such crazy, mixed-up thoughts about our country. Am I the only one who feels this way?
- I don't even go to church anymore because I can't find anyone who believes as I do.
- I am so disappointed in what I hear is the Christian point of view in the media. It is not my point of view, and I don't think it represents God's values in any way.

All of these women are very precious. They have legitimate longings for love. Newborns thrive with love and attention, and being nurtured and cared for is a deep and real longing for adults as well. There are physical consequences to our health when we bear the stress of loneliness for long periods of time. Our bodies show reactions from headaches to stomachaches, with sleeplessness and irritability often increasing as difficulties continue.

Loneliness is actually a dangerous emotional storm that can create deep wounds. Humans were made to thrive in the context of real community. Being deprived of the oxygen of love, belonging, and affirmation slowly snuffs out the very life energy from a person. Scripture tells us, "Two are better than one. . . . Woe to the one who falls when there is not another to lift him up!" (Ecclesiastes 4:9–10).

That had been me—no one to lift me up. We cannot and were not made to face the barrage of the storms of life alone.

When the Hebrew believers, who had been passionate and committed Christians, experienced harsh treatment, rejection, and dire consequences for their beliefs, many were leaving their new faith in Christ and returning to the laws and works of Judaism. The writer of Hebrews warned them, "And let us consider how to stir up one another to love and good works, not neglecting to meet together, as is the habit of some, but encouraging one another, and all the more as you see the Day drawing near" (10:24–25 ESV).

Don't neglect meeting together during difficult times. Sometimes, "difficult" is the best descriptor for normal life! Be intentional and creative about getting together, even if it is a play date with the kids in the park, over the phone with a friend who lives out of state, a cup of coffee before your Bible study, or on a Zoom call with a cup of tea in hand. Take initiative to encourage one another, all the time, especially as we see the coming of Christ drawing nigh.

There is also the Titus 2 verse about older women teaching the younger about motherhood, marriage, and all the rest.

Older women likewise are to be reverent in their behavior, not malicious gossips nor enslaved to much wine, teaching what is good, so that they may encourage the young women to love their husbands, to love their children, to be sensible, pure, workers at home, kind, being subject to their own husbands, so that the word of God will not be dishonored.

Titus 2:3–5

It was very difficult for me to find older women who wanted to invest in me or take time to teach or encourage me about how to deal with all the issues of my life. If I am honest, very few women, when I observed their lives, had my ideals or values, and there were few I would want to influence my life. Many an older woman told me I was too idealistic, and that I just needed to be "like everyone else" (whatever that meant). While there were plenty of women to discourage me from holding on to the biblical ideals I was seeking to live by, it was rare to find someone who would walk the journey with me and show me how to live these ideals in a sustainable way with the experienced wisdom they had gained in life. But I knew I desperately needed a friend to share my burdens, doubts, insecurities, fears, and struggles.

We cannot and were not made to face the barrage of the storms of life alone.

The Importance of Friends

I was thinking recently about how often I have felt alone or dry both spiritually and emotionally, but when I entered into the company of several particular friends, I left feeling stronger, encouraged, with more hopeful and true thoughts about life and the Lord to feed on. These are rare women who have an intentionality about their spiritual lives, and so I know when I invest time with them, I will be investing in my own spiritual well-being.

Friendship is so important as part of our strategy against darkness. Don't go it alone! Often, women say to me, "No one ever invites me over or calls me." It would be so nice if others were intentional, if we could rely on someone else being the first to reach out. But over many years, I have learned that if we wait for others to invite us to be part of something, we may wait for a very long time. Friendships don't usually just happen on their own. Most of the community I now have has happened as a result of my calling people, inviting them to gatherings in my home, and putting forth effort to make memories with women who inspire me. I see it much like planting a garden. When I till the soil and plant the seeds of love, encouragement, thoughtfulness, and reaching out, the flowers of friendship just naturally grow.

> *Friendship is so important as part of our strategy against darkness.*

In looking to form friendships, I have looked for women who are above me in age, who are wiser and cultivate in me a desire to love God more. I call them, take them out, invite them over—because I know what they sow in the garden of my soul will yield beautiful results. Next, I look for peers, women who are at my stage of life, who share the same issues and needs. I have two prayer partners in the same stage of life as me. One calls me every day and we just pray for each other and find out how each of us is doing. The other friend comes to my house once a week and we go walking along a beautiful trail nearby, and after we have caught up on life, we pray for each other.

Finally, I love spending time with women who are younger than I. Young women who are cultivating their ideals bring fresh and vibrant beauty to my soul and offer me a place to sow seeds for the future. Being with younger people helps me stay young!

All of these wonderful friendships started with a plan, a plan to make room and intentionally invite these women into my life with a purpose—because I needed accountability and love. We all hunger for love and friendship and intimacy. We want to know there are people who care for us and really care about us because we are worthwhile and valued.

Family as Close Friends

The older they became, the more difficult it was for my children to find kindred spirits. It took them, too, years to find people who would be steadfast friends who shared their dreams and values for life, which is one of the reasons my daughters and I wrote *Girls' Club*, a whole book about the importance of seeking out and cultivating friendship.

Eventually, through long years of searching for friends, I found that my own now-adult children became, in many ways, the friends I was longing for. We did, after all, share one another's values, dreams, favorite foods, recreation, purposes, and thousands of experiences living life through all seasons together, tying our heartstrings to one another. We truly have become BFFs, and I love, love, love spending

HELP, I'M DROWNING

time together whenever life allows. I discovered family was designed to be its own community of deep affection and love that satisfies longings. No one ever told me my own family could be the community I had been seeking all my adult life. This is true even though we now live in different cities all over the world.

Some Ways to Build Friendships

Perhaps loneliness seems a feature of this time of your life, too, as it does for so many women I know. May I encourage you that God does not want you to be alone? I believe He wants you to experience health and companionship.

Here are some ideas I pray will be helpful to you as you pray for and work toward relationships that bring blessing to everyone involved.

Tea and talk times! Let your friends know that once a week/month you will open your home for friendship and fellowship. You light the candles, everyone else brings a snack to share. Choose one or two verses or concepts in advance that you can talk about, and just have a time of sharing hearts together for a couple of hours. You could pray together, too.

Dinner club! Clay and I started a once-a-month potluck with three other families. We take turns meeting at each other's houses for dinner, and close in sharing and prayer. It has given my children a sense of a close, inner circle of people who care for them. You might plan for holidays together, too: Fourth of July, a chili night in the fall, Thanksgiving gatherings, progressive Christmas dinner, etc.

Girls' night! Have a girls' group for your daughters once a month where you gather moms and daughters and plan something fun to do.

Start a Mom Heart Group! Using one of my books, meet regularly, discussing one chapter a week or month, having prayer, sharing your hearts, and developing friendship with those who are like-minded.

Park day! Call some friends and have a regular day to meet at the park with or without lunches to get some energy out and give the mamas a place to talk.

Minister with other families! Find a retirement center, food bank, or homeless shelter and plan to work there together occasionally.

One-on-one dates! Finally, schedule dates alone with your husband and children. Take time to celebrate relationship.

Healthy relationships aren't easy, they aren't automatic, and they aren't without cost. However, they are definitely worth it—and a key component to overcoming trials of darkness in our lives. When we are sad or overwhelmed, a friend has the power to bring light to our hearts, to speak words of encouragement, to pick us up off the ground or from wherever we have fallen. Allowing others to truly see our hearts, to know our struggles and joys, our hopes and fears, is a powerful deterrent to the hopelessness that attempts to overwhelm everyone at times. Being a faithful friend to someone else is another powerful way to dispel darkness!

> *A friend has the power to bring light to our hearts, to speak words of encouragement, to pick us up off the ground.*

An Anchoring
PRAYER

Dear Heavenly Father,

I come to you in the name of Jesus, so grateful that you welcome me and listen to what is on my heart. You know my need for friends, Lord. You know my ideals make me feel isolated and that the tasks I have to do each day keep me so busy that sometimes I cannot find time to spend in conversation with a friend, even if I could find one! It is so hard sometimes to find people who understand me and share my heart and vision of life. Lord, I pray you would help me find those people who would be true friends to me, and help me be a true friend to others. Thank you that you are my Friend. I love you and am so grateful for your love. Amen.

An Anchoring
SCRIPTURE

Where can I go from Your Spirit?
Or where can I flee from Your presence?
If I ascend into heaven, You are there;
If I make my bed in hell, behold, You are there.
If I take the wings of the morning,

And dwell in the uttermost parts of the sea,
Even there Your hand shall lead me,
And Your right hand shall hold me.

PSALM 139:7–10 NKJV

This chapter has focused on loneliness and our legitimate need for human companionship. Yet I also want to point out that God is our constant companion. We are never actually, completely alone. When my friend found herself walking weakly through the doors of the local emergency room, companionless due to the Covid-19 pandemic and not allowed visitors during her stay, I asked if it was hard or frightening for her to be alone during such a stressful time. "Actually," she told me, "I know it seems it would feel that way. But I had such a feeling of peace the whole time, because I knew the truth was, I was never actually alone—God was always there with me, as my friend." Read over this Scripture passage again and note all the places the psalmist noted that God would be with him. Let this truth sink into your heart: regardless of your circumstances, or your lack of present friends, you are never truly alone.

Is loneliness a common feeling for you? Do you have friends you can call on in times of difficulty or joy? How has loneliness shaped your soul?

An Anchoring
ACT

Make a plan today to reach out to another lonely woman to begin shaping a friendship that may last a lifetime—perhaps you will find your own "bosom friend"! A trip to the park to walk and talk, or meeting at a coffee shop, might be just the thing. Make a note of your intention—goals that are written down are much more likely to be achieved.

FOUR

Broken Expectations

High anticipation versus reality
is a recipe for disaster

Sustain me according to Your word, that I may live;
And do not let me be ashamed of my hope.

Psalm 119:116

I don't just wish you rain, Beloved. I wish you the beauty of
storms.

John Geddes, *A Familiar Rain*

Tears spilling down her cheeks, her voice streaming deep frustration, an angry emotional statement quietly slopped out: "My marriage never gets better, no matter what I say or do to try to make it better. My children create havoc in my life on a regular basis. Life is never what I hoped and thought it would be, and I am so weary going on day after day in the same way."

A dear friend, younger than I, was struggling with her own storms one busy afternoon as we walked together. Centuries-old cobblestone streets with narrow sidewalks forced us to make our way to a favorite café single file, she walking just ahead of me to avoid stepping into the road. We were taking a break from work on some ministry projects we were both excited about, and grabbing a coffee and pastry seemed the perfect treat a few hours after lunch. As we meandered along, admiring the picturesque sandstone buildings of the colleges and intricate wrought-iron fences around Oxford's multiple open green spaces, I had probed a bit. Sometimes long walks reveal deep secrets naturally.

Maybe it was easier to discuss difficult things because we weren't eye-to-eye, because slowly her heart opened up, and out spilled her real feelings. Having known each other for years, we'd spent many hours talking about our personal lives and struggles. I knew one of the most difficult areas she faced involved the mental health issues plaguing several in her family. Being mama to a set of many children spread over two decades was tiring. She had younger children who needed daily attention and training, along with the increased work of having all of her older children at home. She felt overwhelmed as she realized giving appropriate guidance and encouragement to her children would be a lifelong, never-ending task.

"Before we were married, my husband said he was interested in ministry. I was excited about what work we would do together, and pictured our family being very close and even reaching out to others around the world together. But the reality I see right now is so much different. He doesn't seem really interested in church and ministry anymore, and I'm doing most all the work at home with the children. He isn't interested in continuing counseling, and his own issues have not been addressed. I feel alone, isolated, as those issues prevent him from communicating with anyone on a truly deep, personal level. We have continuing financial difficulties, which I can't seem to overcome. Sometimes I just feel like I'm getting more and more sad as life continues, and I worry that my sadness must be obvious to my children. Then I feel even worse because I've piled guilt about my reactions on top of all the negative feelings I have from my difficult situations!"

She took a deep breath and went on as we made our way around streetlights and various people walking the other direction. "So many people have given me advice over the years. Early in our marriage, a pastor's wife offered me a book suggesting all kinds of manipulative ways to get my husband to do what I wanted him to do—in a 'Christian' way, of course. That didn't work.

"Other well-intentioned, eager advisors suggested that if I were just silent and never expressed my disappointment or feelings about difficult situations to him, he would miraculously see his flaws and repent. What false advice that was! No accountability at all. Just more frustration. That obviously didn't work, either.

"Some suggested counseling, but when we met with different leaders at church it just seemed to lead to being pushed out of ministry, and even having our personal lives discussed in gossip—a lesson learned in not trusting people in authority."

She shook her head. "I have tried everything everyone suggested—every kind of prayer, every way of acting—and I've read a zillion books about marriage, and I just can't seem to make this any better. If I'm honest, I feel pretty angry about it all. My kids would be better off if our marriage was better, and it seems like my lifelong dreams for helping other people are handicapped by this situation. We don't fight in front of anyone, or really at all—but we also aren't as strong as I wish we were, you know?" Her voice quivered. "My life just feels like a giant bundle of disappointment some days, and after so many years, I've given up on finding a way to change anything."

"My life just feels like a giant bundle of disappointment some days."

"Maybe that's for the best because it's an acceptance of reality, but it's hard, too. I used to have all these plans for making him change, and in that, somehow there was hope I'd stumble on the right thing. Now I've realized that's really not an option, so I've given up. It seems like all I'm left with is resentment, and I'm mad at God, too. Did He let me make a huge mistake? Why doesn't He make my husband change? Why am I stuck? I feel pretty miserable."

When You Want to Give Up

Before you read the rest of this chapter, I want to assure you that I know some people's lives contain dangerously challenging circumstances. With the wisdom of seasoned advisors and counselors, decisions to take a permanent break or a temporary time of pulling away from a relationship may be necessary in order to live a healthy life. And this need to make hard decisions may also require great faith and wisdom. Such stories do not mean one should feel self-condemnation. God can redeem any life, any story.

But, at the outset, I want to communicate that feeling like you want to quit does not necessarily mean you should. I was not as mature or as wise as I should have been to face the stress and strain that came my way. But I never felt a release from God to leave the stress, to abandon the difficulties in which I found myself. I learned the great value of pushing through. I am even shocked now to see that God was producing fruitfulness in my life beyond my imagina-

Feeling like you want to quit does not necessarily mean you should.

tion by helping me to keep going on His path, one step at a time. Endurance and perseverance by faith can lead to a treasure of blessings when the path is directed and companioned by God.

Consider Olympic champions. They must work diligently, practice over countless years, take correction, and persevere when they feel like quitting. Yet, the one who keeps going forward is the one who might indeed win the gold medal. A medal cannot be won by one who quits amidst the challenging course of becoming excellent. And so it is with life. If we quit circumstances prematurely, we might miss the great rewards that God had stored for us to experience as we cross over our own finish line.

The best part of learning to endure through difficult seasons is the legacy I now see in the lives of my four children. They watched our responses of keeping growing, keeping faithful, growing stronger, and becoming wiser over many years. Now they are standing on our shoulders because our attempted faithfulness has gifted them with wisdom and courage to keep pushing for excellence in their own lives. Heroic endings come as a result of pushing through seemingly impossible times.

Everyone Experiences Disappointment

I nodded my head in understanding and sympathy as I talked with my friend. Marriage can be a place of deep sadness, unfulfilled expectations, and loneliness. Seasons of my life have come and gone. Walking through all of the ups and downs in these areas is where I learned to find secrets of wisdom when I was quiet and desperate, helpless in my own life. Eventual contentment was hard learned over many years of practice. Believing God to be good in spite of how I was feeling or experiencing life pushed me to stretch and reach toward some answers I so needed in my life. In the quiet of sitting humbly with my limitations before Him, I began to find "peace that passed understanding" (see Philippians 4:7). There was insight and perspective to be discovered in unexpected places, light hidden in the corners of darkness, and God's purposes being worked out when I did not understand

There was insight and perspective to be discovered in unexpected places, light hidden in the corners of darkness, and God's purposes being worked out when I did not understand.

but kept walking with Him. Wisdom comes over time, over waiting, over enduring through decades.

My life has not been what I thought it would be. All of our lives are disappointing in some way if we are honest enough to admit it. Every life imperfect, every life affected by the broken world that we live in as well as our own selfishness and self-absorption. One thing I know. There is no perfect family or perfect marriage. Working in ministry for over forty-five years has been greatly disappointing many times, yet dealing with these issues honestly has produced humility I could not have learned any other way, sympathy for other strugglers, and peace in spite of all of my difficult days. Little by little, God unfolded my hands that were holding fast to the things I wanted and thought I needed and opened my hands to the rest He wanted me to experience in the midst of my every day.

I had to learn, and I learned from years and years of growing through experience. Being an intentional mother is harder than I could have imagined, and a longer journey than I expected. Staying faithful and giving up my rights in marriage is incredibly more challenging than I had originally dreamed. Finances are continually difficult as there is no end in sight of our need to eat, buy clothes and cars, live in homes that are in good repair, and have a little extra to celebrate life. Sometimes good church community is hard to find, plans have a tendency to fall apart, and the world seems bent on self-destruction. Global threats such as environmental issues, economic collapse, disease, and a myriad of other problems are beyond my control, yet affect my life day by day. Though this might sound depressing, realistically understanding the nature of this world prepares us to go forward.

Preparation Makes All the Difference

Recently, I returned home to Colorado from the UK for a few weeks for a short furlough. Snowstorms bombarded my mountain town as the temperatures feel well below zero degrees. Because this is a normal occurrence where I live, life went on as usual and most were safe inside the walls of their homes.

You see, we are prepared and armed with snow trucks that clear the roads and drop gravel and salt for safe travel. The pipes in our homes have been drained and wrapped for winter so that they will not burst in frigid weather. Our heating systems are chosen to keep us warm during such times. And we all have snow shovels in our garage to clear our driveways and sidewalks.

However, when the same storm bombarded the southern part of the United States days later and dropped huge amounts of snow, because the land was not suited or prepared for snowstorms, the storm created havoc, devastation, and death. There were no highway vehicles to clear the snow, and pipes burst and created flooding in homes, which caused a dangerous water shortage. Many died from hypothermia, homes were destroyed by bursting pipes, fires broke out in multiple housing developments due to the overexertion of the heating systems, and chaos consumed the area for days.

When we are armed and prepared, storms will not overcome us.

One area fared well through the storms; the other was crippled. And so it is with us. When we are armed and prepared with an expectation of life-storms, have equipped ourselves to endure the chaos, and have ways of staying strong, storms will not overcome us. If I had been armed and ready for what would surely come, knowing all of life would include some elements of battle through the darkness, I might not have struggled as much. But I was not prepared or trained to confront the demands of real-life storms. I had few support systems, and fewer wise mentors. I certainly had no realistic expectation of what marriage and motherhood and ministry would require of me. I just supposed that I would easily be happy and that I would handle the struggles gracefully.

Well . . . that was a nice idea! Broken expectations, though, tend to blindside us. I think disappointment often feels deeper than loneliness or exhaustion, which seem more external somehow. Disappointment strikes at our very hearts.

Don't Let Circumstances Determine Your Happiness

My friend and I finally arrived at the coffee shop that day and bundled into a booth in a back corner with our steaming cups. Looking into her eyes and patting her arm, I said, "Everything you're talking about really is hard. I understand your disappointment. And I have walked through these places with you for years as you have walked with me. But you are going to have to decide something." She looked hopefully at me, raising her eyebrows in question. I took a deep breath and went on. "You are going to have to decide to stop making other people and circumstances responsible for your happiness. Life will always be filled with difficulties, needs, and disruptions. People are imperfect, needy, and limited. Disappointment occurs regularly in life. If you keep expecting and depending on your life to be different, you might always be frustrated. Have you ever heard the saying, "To do the same thing over and over again and to expect different results is lunacy"? Her eyes widened as the words sank in, and then her deep sadness gave way to tears.

"Wait," she whispered, looking around to make sure no one was overhearing us. "Is that what I'm doing?"

"I think so." She nodded, and I went on. "You have to take charge of your life and your happiness, your story right where you are. No one can make you happy, but you have a choice to cultivate joy in every action, every decision, every moment. Cultivating joy and contentment is a work of life, only allotted to those who are willing to search for them, embrace them, celebrate them, find them.

"The circumstances you've been given are your unique puzzle. You must find a way to put the pieces together and bring cohesiveness to it. What if your husband is never perfect and your children disappoint and you fail, and you continue to have a lot of issues to deal with that are hard? What if these things never change? How will you live? Will you be a victim to your uncontrollable circumstances, or can you pursue a path of growing acceptance with grace, happiness that is beyond your circumstances? Can you arm yourself ahead of time with attitudes, rhythms of life that bring grace, a determination to create beauty amidst it all, even if nothing changes? If so, you will construct a place of goodness, redemption, and life with the pieces you are holding in your own hands.

"You're going to have to figure out how to be happy, to find sustainability and contentment in your actual life, just as it is."

Good thing we had sweet almond croissants and warm coffee to temper the edge of reality!

"You start by wrestling with God as you follow Him, learning to submit to the limitations of your life, loving generously, forgiving abundantly, looking for His fingerprints every day, with the grace of a thankful heart. It's going to have to come from hope in God's faithfulness to you, that He is good, that your perseverance matters, and not anything else."

The Heartbreak of Broken Expectations

The bombarding snowstorms I mentioned above regularly change my plans. I have to cancel dinners with friends, move professional meetings on the calendar, and change my schedule. Knowing I will be at home for some days, I have to determine to find productivity inside until the snow melts and life gets back to normal. These storms feel like a metaphor for much of life to me. It's similar to the distance between my ideals and dreams of shaping a wonderful home, getting along with people in my work, and developing meaningful relationships, versus the reality of sick children, fussing between siblings, and all the usual messes that often take me by surprise.

Just when I think I have finally subdued my life, a storm hits and threatens to overwhelm me. And I have found life with adult children has its own challenges, as the issues they face now are not less but (of course!) greater, with greater consequences both positive and negative.

Part of the problem is that we expect to control life, to tame the tempest of every day. Yet if this is our goal, we will always be disappointed because the storms will just keep coming. We live in homes where the laws of thermodynamics can be seen every day—energy is depleting at a constant rate, and everything is moving toward disorder! Our children are selfish and sinful, our husbands are fallible and imperfect just like us; things fall apart, get broken, and cost money; people are unloving; the culture around us is challenging; and we lack support systems to hold up our ideals. Some years ago, I wrote:

> Often it seems we would rather have another life—any life— than our own. Somehow we think if we lived a different life, it would be easier for us to grow in faithfulness and spiritual character. Yet it is in accepting today with all of its issues, in accepting God's will and training grounds that we learn the secret of joy in his presence. It is in being faithful to our own set of tests that we become mature and fitted for the ministry he has called each of us to accomplish.[1]

All our homes are broken, our children are broken, we ourselves are broken, but this is where we must find the personal reality of God. He always loves us, His light is always here for the finding, His wisdom is to be discovered as we invite the Spirit to live through us every day, year after year.

All our homes are broken, our children are broken, we ourselves are broken, but this is where we must find the personal reality of God.

Perhaps this chapter seems a bit negative. Yet, I think often we carry illusions that our lives should be prosperous and have Cinderella endings. We look for easy formulas to figure out how to make life behave. We want escape when in actuality, moving through our circumstances and working hard, learning lessons of life through experience and staying steadfast are where truly valuable stories are formed and character is made.

I believe and have seen that with God on our side, our labor is not in vain but is part of a story of His power and goodness throughout eternity. Feeling weary, discouraged, inadequate, or guilty—or even having all those feelings at the same time—is a normal part of life. Yet, I found that by perceiving myself as His servant, I arm myself with readiness to face another storm. I prepare myself to grow strong so that others may rely upon me to help. One of my goals is to bring God's constant love and redemption into my world as part of the work of walking through my days with Him.

The Life Lessons of Broken Expectations

I think weathering all of these storms taught me the reality of my own deep personal need for God. The difficulties revealed my longing for true, soul-deep satisfaction. I learned the miracle of His life coming into each circumstance to redeem each of my moments. As a young woman, I had committed my life to God. As a growing woman, I slowly understood how profoundly I needed Him. I began to look at life from His eyes and saw how willing He was to flood His light and truth into all of my days. Through this, and because of the storms, He became my treasure.

Engaging in home life, marriage, ministry, and the discipleship of my children was truly the training ground where little by little I learned what it meant to become a more mature Christian. If we run from storms, we avoid learning and growing, we preemptively give up on marriage, family life, and conflict, we prematurely prohibit ourselves from having

God's very life carved into the deep heart and soul places of our lives. The difficult circumstances of my life presented a challenge to mount up over and through and develop a habit of trust by practicing it. It also taught me to find my joy every day—not dependent on circumstances, but on the reality of His music and light dancing through my heart.

Choose to Live Life Joyfully

My world is always a mixture of beauty and mess, order and piles of things not yet subdued. Did I mention that a child has interrupted me three times since I started writing this chapter? My adult children still call, want help, need advice, and just want my companionship—and then there is my husband! Yet, I find significance in a little wooden plaque within eye range. It reminds me daily, "Live Life Joyfully!" We have the agency to make choices of how we will live life. We also have capacity to become stronger, wiser, and more compassionate for other strugglers. But it requires us to choose to strain forward to God's righteousness and truth. Over a period of many years, I have learned to choose to live life joyfully by choosing to submit my attitudes and emotions into His hands. Choosing to enjoy the moment is an inner discipline in which spiritual muscles grow from practice. It is not necessarily natural, but it has become more so as I choose it as my practiced heart attitude.

I love to watch toddlers. They move through their worlds with delight. Years ago on a mission trip, we were waiting in a park for a friend to meet us. A towheaded little boy was squealing with delight as he chased an elusive butterfly around a planting of bright red tulips and yellow daffodils.

He was caught up in the joy of the moment, delighting in the seeming toy figures that God had placed in the world just for his pleasure. The little one was unaware that he had a milk mustache, a shoe untied, and a stain on the knee of his jeans.

I hope that I am like this little boy to God—choosing to enjoy the beauty of the treasures He has placed in my path. Cultivating joy is a strategic part of the battle, noticing the gifts He has granted me for delight. I am even convinced that God created

Cultivating joy is a strategic part of the battle.

golden retrievers just for our pleasure—they are furry balls of love who follow us everywhere with an easygoing attitude, pretty much saying, "You need some affection? I am here to provide that!"

I remember mornings recently with Joy dancing through my room, asking me to practice Spanish with her, while I was writing this book with a demanding deadline. She was truly a beautiful sight to behold and a snapshot of delight to cherish. Daily, I intentionally look at her when I have the privilege of having her at home. It is a miracle to me that she still enjoys the company of her mama. But I had to look at the moment with eyes of thankfulness rather than thinking of her as an interruption to my life. I don't have her with me often now. She lives in Scotland, finishing her PhD, and has an independent adult life far away from me. This fun interruption passed quickly, yet the fragrance of her love stays with me.

As I look out the window, I am enjoying the mums on my next-door neighbors' driveway, and the green grass so long hidden under piles of rain and snow. Living into the possibility of the joy of God and bringing it to others is an intentional, purposeful way of seeing, a grid through which I have learned to view my life.

Many years ago, in the midst of another possible miscarriage, I was sitting by a window near some mountains in Austria. I had begun to bleed, again, at five months and was asking God from the bottom of my heart to please let me carry this child to completion.

Just then, a little sparrow hopped up on my windowsill and began to chirp. It stayed there for several minutes and hopped closer and closer to the edge where I was looking out. What a sweet, amazing creature—singing its heart out with no one to applaud. It was as though God was saying to me, "I am listening. My eye is on the sparrow. I see you. I love you and am with you!" I still didn't know what would happen, but I was overwhelmed with a sense of His presence. I knew that God, who is love, was with me and would be with me in whatever happened.

The pregnancy turned out to be Sarah, my oldest child.

From then on, I decided to take notice of birds that sing—to believe that they are especially praising God. I see them also as a personal reminder from God that He is present. Often on my walks when I am pouring out my dark heart to God, a bird hops or sings along my trail and I am reminded that God is there—present with me! May He bring the reality of His joy to you today in the midst of your order and mess.

Moving Past Discouragement and Disappointment

The key to making it through the storms of disappointment or discouragement is not to pretend they don't exist. So often we fall into the trap of believing something we're engaged in or hoping for has the power to fulfill a deep longing or need we have, yet when we finally obtain the thing or situation or position or person we wanted, we find it disappointingly inadequate. Often, we think our lives are too small and if we had another scenario, we would be more fulfilled. Yet, in order to work through our depression, we must put our finger on the sources that have caused the heart anger and frustration. To move past the disappointment we may feel over the smallness of our lives, we have to develop a more long-range view, open to possibilities we may never see.

You might as well decide to like God's will, because it is not going to change, and you have to find peace within it.

We all find ourselves characters who have been set into unique, complicated stories, surrounded by other unique, complicated people. Some of the cards we have been dealt are pleasing, and some just drive us crazy. I have often told my children what I've told myself: "You might as well decide to like God's will, because it is not going to change, and you have to find peace within it."

We often struggle with His will because we find the characters we are surrounded by and the stories we are set in to be unacceptable, embarrassing, and less than perfect. And of course, everything is more difficult when we believe (or realize) we ourselves fit those same negative descriptions sometimes.

Years ago, I was feeling overwhelmed and discouraged by a difficult situation with a certain member of our family who seemed to be complicating much of life. As I was praying about it all one afternoon, I came across Psalm 37:8, which reads, "Refrain from anger and turn from wrath; do not fret—it leads only to evil" (NIV).

Suddenly I realized that is exactly what I was doing—fretting. I was thinking about the situation over and over, rehearsing all the things that had gone or could ever go wrong, and all the difficulties which ensued, and all the negative results that could happen over the decades stretching before me. Yet God's Word was so clear in saying fretting would not lead to anything positive, only evildoing. Fretting is a waste of time, and it does not bring grace, peace, or love into a circumstance.

Women can be so prone to worry and fuss and be uptight; at least, this woman can be. I wish at a much earlier age I had learned to chill more, to dance more, to stop and smell the flowers. I wish I had not been such a people pleaser, trying to live up to the expectations of my extended family, my critics, or my peers. My family puzzle just did not fit into the pattern of others' expectations, so trying to live up to those unrealistic standards was impossible. I wish I had accepted that at the very first, instead of fretting about things I could not change. But I did learn. Daily, my habit is to practice being thankful, to encourage all who come into my path, if possible, and to celebrate the moments of life by bringing beauty into them.

Discouragement comes when we feel hopeless to change a circumstance (or a person) who is less than what we wish it (or they) would be. Yet this is often the price of maturity, realizing we can only control our own thoughts and behavior and our reactions to other people. We are not all-powerful, even in cases of people who would obviously be better off were they to take our advice! And since everyone we are surrounded by is dealing with the same sin nature we are, they will often act in ways that will leave us feeling disappointed in them.

One doesn't find peace until she relinquishes her rights and her disappointed expectations and learns to rest in the place where she finds herself. To have peace and rest within our lives, we must die to ourselves, letting go of our failures, our disappointments, and our broken expectations. We must hold out our hands to God just as a toddler would hold out their little arms to a parent, and say, "I need your help, Lord."

Seeing us as His own beloved children, He will welcome us into His arms and honor us with His wisdom, soothing our restlessness and dis-ease. He will whisper gently to us the secrets of a happy life, giving us His perspective on our very own. He is indeed in the boat with us. Hope comes when we let go of our own expectations and watch for what He is actually doing within our actual lives and wait for His conclusion, knowing He will indeed bring us safely out of the storm.

An Anchoring
PRAYER

Heavenly Father,

I am so grateful I can come to you in full confidence in the name of Jesus. You see my heart and you know my disappointments. Lord, I don't want to fight against the story I am in. Please help me to accept this plot, this setting, these characters. Help me to trust that you are working good things, even when I cannot see them. Please lift my spirit toward you, allowing me to see from your point of view. Forgive where I have become bitter in any way toward you, or toward those I've seen as hindering my own purposes. Help me lay down my desire to change others, and help me find happiness in bringing you joy. May I continue to serve and love and be faithful in small and difficult places, knowing you are pleased with that humble perseverance. You are good to me, Lord. Remind me of that goodness and help me to hope in it today, once again. I love you.

An Anchoring
SCRIPTURE

"For I know the plans I have for you," says the LORD. "They are plans for good and not for disaster, to give you a future and a hope."

JEREMIAH 29:11 NLT

We can sometimes read or hear a particular Scripture so many times, we don't really hear what it says anymore. Please go back and read this one again.

What rises in your heart as you read? Is this easy for you to believe, or difficult? Why?

What are some of the plans you can see God having for you?

An Anchoring
ACT

Find a quiet place where you can sit with your hands open on your knees, and say something like this to God:

Lord, please help. There are broken expectations, disappointments, and discouragement in my life. I need your love, grace, joy, and peace today. Help me to see your presence in this place in time, in these circumstances, within my own limitations. Open my eyes to beauty, to your fingerprints personally around me today.

Listen to what He may impress upon your heart in response and write it down.

FIVE

Busyness + Distraction = Exhaustion

Everything is a problem when you're worn out

Come to Me, all who are weary and burdened, and I will give you rest. Take My yoke upon you and learn from Me, for I am gentle and humble in heart, and you will find rest for your souls. For My yoke is comfortable, and My burden is light.

Matthew 11:28–30

If patience is worth anything, it must endure to the end of time. And a living faith will last in the midst of the blackest storm.

Mahatma Gandhi

It was a hot summer morning in Colorado, and I was exhausted.

After listening to my laments about dragging myself out of bed every morning, struggling through the day, and having barely enough energy to make dinner after long days of mothering a busy four-year-old and almost three teenagers, a friend had heard enough. She kindly suggested perhaps I should talk to someone who might be able to get to the bottom of the issue and recommended a doctor she knew.

Thankfully, another friend agreed to keep all my children at her home during my appointment. Doing my best to get everyone settled, I finally headed to the door with one child clinging to my leg and two more asking "When will you be back?" for the twenty-fifth time. I sighed deeply and gave a few more hugs, reassuring everyone I'd be back very soon while my friend and I exchanged knowing looks.

By the time I was actually on my way, my mind was racing. Two book deadlines were bearing down on me, and fatigue made it difficult to focus early in the morning or late at night, which is when I was most likely to find some quiet. Clay was working extra hours and never home as much as I wish he could be. (Don't most wives feel life is always this way?) In my mid-forties, my hormones seemed to be going berserk just as my teens entered their own angsty seasons, which made for way too much testosterone and estrogen in our house. On top of all this, I was experiencing pain in my stomach and an occasional fever, which was worrying me.

The doctor seemed to be about my age and looked disapprovingly at me as I listed my symptoms. He ran a battery of tests, then asked what my daily life was like. I explained that needing to find quiet time to work meant I was often up early and went to bed late, spending most of the day on my feet except when I was frantically trying to find a few more moments to jot down a new idea or answer a mom's questions on the phone, chasing a toddler, and driving my teens to work and various gatherings with friends for classes and lessons. He left the room shaking his head. When he had my results in hand, he crossed his arms over his chest, peered over his glasses down his nose at me, and said, "Well, you can die early if you want to by keeping up this pace. Or are you willing to change some of your priorities?"

That was quite a wake-up call. As I thought over my life, changing my priorities sounded great—only my children weren't likely to let me stop making meals and washing laundry, and unfortunately, the bathrooms weren't exactly going to clean themselves! I sighed and thanked him, though I wasn't sure how to practically make this prescription happen. It was then that I began to realize that no one else was going to take responsibility for my health and well-being. I, as a mature adult, needed to monitor my life and have a plan for rejuvenating, or apparently the consequences were going to be serious. I put some practices into place at that time, which did help, and obviously

I began to realize that no one else was going to take responsibility for my health and well-being.

I did not die! However, exhaustion has continued to be a constant challenge over the ensuing decades of my life. But I realized that this storm was self-created. I could blame no one else for my exhaustion and "brown-out" state of mind. I was the only one who could be responsible for the well-being of my heart, mind, body, soul.

Why Are We All So Tired?

We live in a culture of go-go-go, with pressure to perform, produce, and impress constantly weighing on us. Yet we aren't made for exhaustion, and when we experience it, everything in life seems more difficult to deal with. What is it about contemporary life that tends to leave us feeling so sapped, across the board?

It's just hard

So much of the problem for women is simply the reality of life with others—children, roommates, husband, family! We often find ourselves in caretaking roles, where we feel pressure to be the ideal wife, mother, friend, and co-worker. If you're a mom, you know the task of "ideal" mothering is simply a truly tiring calling, one that may require the use of all our resources twenty-four hours a day for many, many years. If we also take into account that we have similar responsibilities as women yet such different personalities, the issue makes even more sense.

We may find that we have particular areas that seem to amplify our exhaustion. If there is one area of family life that takes the breath out of me, personally, it is simple housework. The relentlessness of it is probably my biggest source of stress. I was never taught how to keep house or how to cook or wash clothes or organize as a child; the work just seemed to happen magically in my home. I never took notice of how everything got done. While I am great at decorating and building ambiance in our home, Clay is naturally much better at organizing the house than I will ever be, so all the things that have to be kept in order and the details of the fridge, the wash, the bills, the toys, and the papers—well, you get the picture—these are just too much for me, and can leave me depleted and despairing, so it's good (and rare, too) that Clay doesn't mind helping, at least sometimes.

Here's what I know: God gave me my personality with its limitations and gifts, and He isn't biting His nails to see if I am going to be perfect at every task, or finish everything on time, even if my publisher or the neighbors are setting a high bar for what is expected of me. Knowing that He knows my limitations takes a little pressure off. A perfect house is not what is expected. As Joel, my son, once said when I was in a tizzy over the messy house, "Mom, we can all jump up and work hard now, and we will get the house all clean— but it will just get messy again. The problem is, when you are upset about it being messy, we feel guilty, like we have done something wrong. But when you are happy, we feel happy, and like we are the greatest family in the world. So, Mom, just lighten up, and we will all be okay!"

Knowing that He knows my limitations takes a little pressure off.

I think Joel has the right idea. Sometimes we just need to realize that we're tired because we are working very hard, and that's okay. Sometimes we need to realize we're tired because we're working too hard, and we're making everyone around us miserable, and that's not okay.

Comparison

Years ago, I had written on my blog a story about taking Nathan for lunch and a hike, then inviting his friends over, plus planning a trip with Joy for her birthday. A dear one who meant to send a private comment to her friend in response accidentally pushed the reply button, which sent her email to me, instead. It read, "She makes me tired!" So many mamas who share their lives and stories tell me that they, too, are often overwhelmed and fatigued by their own busy lives, but also by the constant comparison to others' seemingly flourishing lives online.

We all put ourselves under so much pressure to be perfect when we have sinful children, imperfect husbands, few or no support systems, no breaks, no full-time maids, and our kids all want to eat and wear reasonably clean clothes every day! Of course, it is also a lot to ask of one human when we deem ourselves responsible for their character, manners, education, spiritual input, sense of well-being, and happiness, too.

We have to remind ourselves that comparison can amplify exhaustion and depression. Comparison is always a losing game, because if the person we're looking at seems to be doing poorly, pride may cause us to judge and criticize them. Conversely, a person who has a life that appears to be in order can elicit a response of insecurity if we feel we just cannot measure up. Comparison never accomplishes anything positive in the long run, and thank goodness, God does not judge us by someone else's arbitrary standard, even though we may have many voices in our heads telling us otherwise.

God does not judge us by someone else's arbitrary standard.

Giving out without taking in

Do you ever find yourself exhausted, but feeling you don't have a real reason to feel that way? Not really knowing what's wrong, but having a sense of lethargy, no energy or motivation, like you'd rather go back to bed than take on the projects of your day? Perhaps you feel far away from God and don't know exactly why. Some call it burnout. Some blame it on their age or hormones. Some just think it is inevitable with too much activity—or, in what seems an odd contradiction, boredom. Either way, it's not a healthy way to live or a pleasant way to experience life, and it's not the model we want to live out in front of our children.

We women are dispensing time, attention, love, and effort at a much faster rate than we are generally receiving those things, so depletion and exhaustion are normal, though not optimal. Proverbs 14:4 tells us, "Where there are no oxen, the manger is clean; but much revenue comes by the strength of the ox." I'm not so sure about the "much revenue" part, but I do know that my house/manger is cleaner when there aren't quite so many oxen around!

A pitcher of water can only pour out what has first been poured into it.

However, I like my oxen and miss them now that they are gone much of the time.

There's a natural law in effect here: a pitcher of water can only pour out what has first been poured into it. Once empty, the vessel is unable to produce water on its own; no matter how long it is held in a position of pouring, no more refreshment will emerge to pour into others until it has itself been refreshed. We would do well to look at ourselves with the same understanding.

The emotional exhaustion of discouragement

There have been several seasons in my life when I've felt it—that creeping tiredness that seemed to seep into my very bones. Weariness as I hear another story of a wife betrayed, a child left to his own devices and finding himself in trouble, a pastor abandoning his flock or being fired because of adultery, global financial issues, teenagers in general. Discouragement over a long to-do list that looks just like the one I *almost* finished yesterday. Resentment over the feeling of never having a moment to myself.

I can find my self-talk sounding a tad like Eeyore. On a busy day I echo him:

> "Everybody crowds round so in this Forest. There's no Space. I never saw a more Spreading lot of animals in my life, and all in the wrong places."[1]

And then when things quiet down and I'm left alone?

> "One can't complain. I have my friends. Somebody spoke to me only yesterday. And was it last week or the week before that Rabbit bumped into me and said 'Bother!' The Social Round. Always something going on."[2]

It's only funny when I can look back on how I felt like Eeyore yesterday—not so much when I'm actually feeling the emotions that make me want to say those things! Then, I realize perhaps I've drifted a bit. When the pressures of life are great and negatives loom large, they sometimes take up more room in my vision than they should. A readjustment is in order. I must get back to my first love.

Distraction, too, adds to the problem of exhaustion. There are the everyday interruptions that have been typical of life for generations: the car that breaks down on the way to a meeting, the phone call from a family member during an important conversation with your husband, the toddler who needs to show you something "right now!" More recently, modern pressures of busyness have forced their way in, causing our planners to be filled with all the activities our children expect to take part in, work deadlines, the many hours our churches want us to serve, and our own ideals of workouts, recreation time, date nights, etc., almost before we get them home and break out the pens. I have discovered that you can only fulfill a limited number of ideals at one time. So choose the priorities that suit your personality and the particulars of your own life demands.

A distracted, divided mind leads to an exhausted, empty heart.

I do want to add a caveat. There are seasons (babies who don't sleep, illnesses that last and must be attended to, moving, circumstances beyond our control) when a balanced life is just not possible. We cannot always make life behave, but our response to the difficulties can help us breathe in peace and at least have a restful, trusting heart.

But this century has added an entirely new dimension, the elephant in the room of every discussion on distraction, something our foremothers never could have anticipated: the rise of media in general and the smartphone in particular.

The fact that our minds are moving from one area of focus to another in such a rapid manner on a regular basis in today's culture is costing us more than we are perhaps aware. I cannot count the number of women who have shared with me that their phones hold much more sway over them than they like, interrupting their time with their children as their brains cry out for affirmation or even simply information seemingly more in tune with an adult world. When I asked a group of high schoolers what they wished their moms would change about their day-to-day lives at home, the overwhelming answer was, "I wish she would put down her phone." And that was back in the early 2000s!

Smartphones can make us feel we have the world in our pockets, but we are in danger of losing the one immediately around us because of them. Our brains aren't designed to handle the siren call of the world's billions of people and thousands of companies vying for our attention. Our souls simply don't do well when we are distracted.

> Now as they were traveling along, He entered a village; and a woman named Martha welcomed Him into her home. And she had a sister called Mary, who was also seated at the Lord's feet, and was listening to His word. But Martha was distracted with all her preparations; and she came up to Him and said, "Lord, do You not care that my sister has left me to do the serving by myself? Then tell her to help me." But the Lord answered and said to her, "Martha, Martha, you are worried and distracted by many things; but only one thing is necessary; for Mary has chosen the good part, which shall not be taken away from her."
>
> Luke 10:38–42

Can you picture the scene? Oh, I am sure you can! Who hasn't found themselves in Martha's position at times—an impending deadline at work, important company on the way, the house in a bit of a flurry, Cheerios on the floor in the corner, the dog barking because she doesn't want to go to her spot upstairs, the pantry not as full as we would wish, and where, oh where did we put the coffee tray that would be just perfect with the dessert we wanted to serve?

Recently, as I was preparing for a group of twelve women to join me for dinner, I found myself almost in tears as the kitchen and living room slowly became more and more smoke-filled, because I had decided to try a new recipe (I know, I know) and my oven's vents just could not handle the high heat called for as I pan-fried the chicken, which was the main part of dinner, half an hour before everyone arrived. Thankfully, a nice cherry sauce seemed to make up for the fog that lingered just a bit even after windows had been opened! Someone had offered to bring rolls but then forgot, which meant we had no bread, and the salad dressing wasn't quite as good as the other times I had made it. After we'd finished dinner and I felt the evening had been redeemed as we shared Scripture and gifts in a room full of candles

Our souls simply don't do well when we are distracted.

and atmospheric music, my dog rushed downstairs past one of the boys and promptly got sick on the carpet right in the midst of everyone!

Martha may have been having one of these days, too. Scripture says Jesus had come, along with His disciples, to the home she shared with her sister, Mary, and brother, Lazarus. There is no mention of fathers or husbands here, so it is possible that Mary and Martha were young orphans, or perhaps even widows who had taken up residency with their brother. As she is most often mentioned first in several biblical accounts, Martha was probably the oldest of the family, and here we see her bustling about, preparing for presumably a fairly large number of guests. She welcomes Jesus into her home, and then, when He sits down and begins to teach those gathered there, she returns to her tasks. Perhaps she was still folding towels or making beds; perhaps there was stew to be stirred or one last dish to wash. At some point, she realizes she is alone, and Mary is sitting at Jesus' feet, listening, as if she hasn't a care in the world—certainly not whether the water for washing has been heated. And Martha is angry.

Luke makes it incredibly clear what bothers Martha: she is "distracted with all her preparations." This story has become the ubiquitous example of the busy hostess, and we often hear it as though we ought to be ashamed of our natural desire to provide and prepare for those to whom we offer hospitality. Yet, surely Jesus and the disciples would be hungry that evening and appreciate a nourishing, delicious dinner with their friends after much travel and discussion. Surely clean towels and blankets would be comforting, and cleanliness has aesthetic as well as health benefits. Note that Jesus doesn't tell her she should not have been doing all those things. He merely points out the truth, that she is "worried and distracted by many things." He does not tell Martha that she should be sitting down instead of working, but neither will he tell Mary to go help her; He commends Mary's choice of sitting at His feet—the one thing that is necessary. Mary is focused; Martha is distracted.

What's So Bad about Being Tired?

Many years ago, I was visiting friends who were missionaries in Europe. As we talked, I began to notice that so many were feeling disillusioned, discouraged in their ministries by a lack of results, difficulties within team relationships, and of course missing everything about their various original homes. I could understand their feelings because I had some of the same challenges and felt the same weight within my own life. As I sat alone in a lovely plaza one afternoon, pausing and pondering all this as I sipped a coffee, I began to think back to years before, when I first learned about the love of Jesus for me.

Unfortunately, I had to admit that I had slowly shifted from the place I had been back then. My friend group at college used to stay up late at night discussing all the epic truths we were learning in the Bible. We prayed fervently and shared what we were learning with strangers on a regular basis. Our fellowship was precious, and I also found myself reading my Bible for hours as I searched for the truths and understanding that was all new to me. The truth was, I was happier then. God was my whole life, and it was exciting, passion-filled, purposeful, and even full of grace for me as well as everyone around me.

Now, though, things seemed to have changed. While I sometimes felt the surge of joy and excitement in my heart over the following decades, it was seldom—and fewer and farther between. Duty drove me forward, and commitment kept me doing what I knew I should do. Cultivating a faithful personal character and living a life of obedience counted for something, and I knew it was good, but doing it all without any emotion to propel all of that work was making me feel more exhausted than inspired. As I sat in the park that day, I realized this wasn't enough. So much more than a list of rules I could write down, a sophisticated philosophy, or a complicated theology, I wanted an intimate, true, deep, breathing relationship with Jesus, the One who had originally called out to my heart.

My friends' malcontent was functioning as a powerful warning, too. Picturing myself entering heaven's gates and finally seeing Jesus, I did not want to do so with a frown on my face, out of breath, gasping, or grouching. I wanted to run to Him with a smile from ear to ear, full of joy and hope and peace—having experienced the satisfaction, joy, and contentedness He died to give me. Surely my longing for those things was an indicator that God wanted more for me than I was currently experiencing. Surely He didn't enjoy my rote, dead obedience any more than I did. Surely the One who crafted giraffes and hot peppers, rainbows and snowflakes, emus and flamingos didn't want me to live life in a state of exhaustion and darkness, but to dance with Him day by day.

Surely the One who crafted giraffes and hot peppers, rainbows and snowflakes, emus and flamingos didn't want me to live life in a state of exhaustion and darkness, but to dance with Him day by day.

And that's what He wants for your life, too. We must find a way to return to our first love if we are to escape the exhaustion trap. I determined that I would draw closer to God and not allow exhaustion to steal my love for Him away. Times of regular rest (Sabbath!) have been the most helpful for me in this battle.

Bottom line is that the only way to get through life with grace is to mount up over the challenges, seeking to live a focused life that fills us a little every day, with a heart that is valiant and unwilling to give in to the woes that tempt us. We have choices to make, a life to tame, but living in the joy of God is possible. We must be intentional about cultivating personal friendships, taking ten-minute tea breaks to breathe, spending time to read a book or ponder life or to write a note to a friend. To sail, so to speak, into the clouds with hope requires planning. But living it out will give us what we need to breathe in God's peace and to rest in His love.

To tiptoe downstairs while the rest of the house is sleeping and engage in a regular time of quiet and privacy, cup of tea in hand, lit candle on the table nearby, my Bible or devotional reading open, and still my heart before God somehow helps both my heart and day expand. I find His strength carrying me through whatever comes, rather than trying to handle it all myself—a sure recipe for exhaustion. This is my daily habit. A few moments in the afternoon for regular teatime has also become routine. When my children were little, I sent everyone to their rooms for an hour or so with a good stack of books and something yummy to eat, giving myself the gift of quiet for just a bit and modeling for them the need for solitude and peace (not to mention reading!).

Every year, I take a weekend or two away to pray and journal my thoughts and plans for the upcoming season. These days of solitude are helpful in themselves. But I also find the act of decluttering and then organizing my soul and schedule helps my tendency toward exhaustion to slowly fade and allows me to plan ways to prevent becoming overwhelmed.

This is the day the Lord has made; we will rejoice and be glad in it.

Psalm 118:24 NKJV

An Anchoring
PRAYER

Dearest Lord,

Here I am again, feeling a bit weary. It seems everyone wants and needs so much from me, and I sometimes wonder if there is enough of me to go around, or whether I'll eventually just disappear because there's nothing left of me to give! Yet I know you know best, and you know the needs all these precious ones have. Some days I feel so bored I just want to go back to bed. There are so many hard things in the world, in my life; I feel inadequate to face it all. Lord, would you be my sufficiency? Will you fill me with strength so I might go on? Help me steady myself before you, quiet my soul, and receive your grace and encouragement. Help me know that my exhaustion can only be healed in your presence, and remind me you are here to be my helper. In the name of Jesus, Amen.

An Anchoring
SCRIPTURE

Unless the LORD builds the house, the builders labor in vain. Unless the LORD watches over the city, the guards stand watch in vain. In vain you rise early and stay up late, toiling for food to eat—for he grants sleep to those he loves.

PSALM 127:1–2 NIV

Read that again!

What feelings does this verse bring up in you? Is it difficult to imagine what it might mean for the Lord to build your house?

How about guarding it?

Do you rise early or stay up late, "toiling"? Ask the Lord what He wants to say about this, and consider His promise to grant you sleep.

An Anchoring
ACT

Spend some time thinking about where in your home is the most restful place to you—perhaps it is a spot in the living room, a comfortable chair on your back porch, or even your own bed. What is one thing you might do to make this space even more restful?

_____

_____

_____

_____

_____

_____

Craven Fear

Cowering in a corner is a hard place to be

Be strong and courageous. Do not be afraid; . . . for the LORD
your God will be with you wherever you go.

Joshua 1:9 NIV

The wise man in the storm prays God not for safety from
danger but for deliverance from fear.

Ralph Waldo Emerson

F ear is indeed one of those ugly giants that wraps its
dark claws around my heart and squeezes at times,
usually coming upon me by surprise and creating
sudden panic. It has attacked me on all fronts but knows my

most vulnerable point is the well-being of my loved ones. Fear reminds me that I am not in control and tempts me to the most extreme thoughts. Do you struggle with sudden fear, too?

Arriving at the home of my eldest daughter after making the move to Oxford, I anxiously scanned her eyes. I saw there the remnants of sickness and resulting weariness still clinging to her after months of fighting an ailment. Dark circles under her eyes and frequent sighing and coughing gave evidence of illness still lingering. Wrapping my arms around her, I felt her draw in a deep breath and murmur, "It's so good to see you—I'm so glad you're here!" As one little grandchild ran to meet me yelling "Queenie! Queenie is here!" I laughed and gathered her into my arms and smiled at the speedy Samuel crawling as fast as he could to join us. I was just as grateful to see them as they were me. I have to admit that though I adore my grandchildren, my daughter—my firstborn—is always a little bit ahead of them, resting in the center of my heart. After all, I am *her* mama.

Somehow, just being there with them dispelled some of the fear I'd been fighting for many weeks. Sarah had been struggling with illness and was only allowed to speak with a physician over Zoom. Aches and pains, fever, and pneumonia that returned three times left her exhausted and bedridden off and on for fifteen weeks. She received a wrong diagnosis (or two?) and multiple rounds of medicine we'd hoped would help but somehow had not brought about the complete eradication of whatever was striking her so hard.

Each time I'd talked with her on the phone over those past weeks, I could feel the fear rising in my heart. When she first became sick, I was still at our home near Colorado Springs, and many travel restrictions due to the pandemic prevented me from going to be with her. In addition, the rules of lockdown in her area meant no one who lived nearby could really do much to help practically, either. From years of listening to her voice, I could tell something wasn't quite right; her breathing was shallow, and she did a lot of coughing if she said more than a sentence or two at a time.

Each time I'd talked with her on the phone, I could feel the fear rising in my heart.

As a lifelong asthmatic, almost dying twice from double pneumonia and having experienced multiple hospitalizations, I knew further congestion in her lungs was dangerous, and whenever we weren't talking I found myself worrying about the situation. What if the pneumonia settled into her lungs and couldn't be eradicated? What if she truly stopped breathing as I had done once as a child, causing me to pass out? What if Thomas (her husband) or the children got sick, too? Worst of all . . . what if Sarah died without me being there? (I am not known for being a small thinker, but like to take every possibility to its farthest extreme.) What if Thomas was lost, too? What would happen to the children? Could we care for them? That seemed quite a task to take on at sixty-eight! Long distance somehow magnifies fears and vain imaginations.

Our visit was wonderful though brief, and being able to serve her as well as spend time reading and playing and baking and walking in the beautiful countryside with my grandchildren brought relief to my worries . . . at least until I had to return home.

Fear upon Fear

As Sarah continued to battle the lingering effects of her illness, I received a call from my assistant in Tennessee; she had Covid-19 herself and was doing poorly. As the days went on and her condition worsened, I urged her to go to the hospital, but her doctor seemed hesitant to take action. I knew my friend would not want to leave her family and would probably try to power through and pretend everything was fine. Her voice sounded just like Sarah's, and each time we talked my concern grew until one day she reported that her oxygen level had dropped so low she was being admitted to the hospital. At least then I could relax a bit, knowing she was being watched over—but what if they just couldn't help?

The year of 2020 was one in which it seemed opportunities for fear were around every corner. A worldwide pandemic hadn't been seen in a hundred years, and it was followed by isolation, job loss, financial crisis, and mental health distress that threw people worldwide into panic. My newlywed son and his wife in New York City reported its streets as empty, the city seeming to have lost its life as restaurants and theatres, concert halls and various gathering venues shut down while hospitals filled. Living in a tiny, utilitarian studio apartment day in, day out did not seem the best way to begin a new marriage. More to worry about.

Then came increased racial tensions after centuries of injustice in America, and peaceful protests followed by anything-but-peaceful rioting in the streets of several cities. One of the members of our ministry team reported buildings being boarded up and families afraid to let their children play outdoors even in the suburban areas surrounding her own large city on the West Coast. The frightening news filled our news feeds even as many were isolated at home with nothing to do but watch, as leaders took sides that confused many and caused others to rethink ideas long held dear—a disconcerting feeling in itself. The devastation continued into 2021 with the violent storming of the Capitol, where legislators had to hide and run for their lives; destruction was rampant, and havoc seemed to reign even more.

I have been through many other storms in my life when I felt I could not go on due to fear. Three out of four of my children were asthmatics with constant illness and emergency room situations; there was stress in finances that looked impossible and put us in difficult straits; ministry, marriage, and "giants" within our family caused great difficulty and despair. Often, I would think, *I cannot go on. My circumstances will turn out for the worst. There is no hope!*

Fear Is a Tool of the Enemy

Panic, worry, cynicism, and frustration seem to define the mood and emotions of many today. Reports indicate that anxiety disorders among children and adults are growing in numbers higher than at any other period of history. When we look out on the world, there are devastating storms, health threats, financial stresses, and fearmongering all about. And yet, it is in the midst of the storms of life

Panic, worry, cynicism, and frustration seem to define the mood and emotions of many today.

that our faith is most precious. It is in these times when we can say to Satan, "You would have me fear, but I choose to believe in the goodness of God and in His provision."

After almost seventy years of subduing the life God has given me, I have walked through my fair share of adventures, joys, and sometimes disasters. One of the worst things the enemy can do is to truly convince us that our situation is unique, that we are completely alone, and that we will never be able to make it out to see the silver lining. While it's easy to believe that we are unique in times of darkness and difficulty, Scripture is filled with stories of people who faced various situations of disaster and destruction, and so are the lives of people throughout history, as well as our neighbors—and the person who looks back at us from the mirror every morning. Stories from Scripture and reading historical nonfiction have helped me stretch toward being strong and brave. The story of Gideon was one such story, as he also lived in a dangerous, turbulent time.

Fear Sometimes Comes from the Attacks of Others

Then the sons of Israel did what was evil in the sight of the LORD; and the LORD handed them over to Midian for seven years. The power of Midian prevailed against Israel. Because of Midian the sons of Israel made for themselves the dens which were in the mountains and the caves and the strongholds. For whenever Israel had sown, the Midianites would come up with the Amalekites and the people of the east and march against them. So they would camp against them and destroy the produce of the earth as far as Gaza, and leave no sustenance in Israel, nor a sheep, ox, or donkey.

For they would come up with their livestock and their tents,
they would come in like locusts in number, and both they
and their camels were innumerable; and they came into the
land to ruin it. So Israel was brought very low because of
Midian, and the sons of Israel cried out to the LORD. . . .
Then the angel of the LORD came and sat under the oak
that was in Ophrah, which belonged to Joash the Abiezrite,
as his son Gideon was beating out wheat in the wine press
in order to save it from the Midianites. And the angel of
the LORD appeared to him and said to him, "The LORD
is with you, valiant warrior." Then Gideon said to him,
"O my lord, if the LORD is with us, why then has all this
happened to us? And where are all His miracles which our
fathers told us about, saying, 'Did the LORD not bring us
up from Egypt?' But now the LORD has abandoned us and
handed us over to Midian." And the LORD looked at him
and said, "Go in this strength of yours and save Israel from
the hand of Midian. Have I not sent you?" But he said to
Him, "O Lord, how am I to save Israel? Behold, my family is
the least in Manasseh, and I am the youngest in my father's
house."

Judges 6:1–6, 11–15

Israel's greatest judge had a rather inauspicious beginning. The chosen people of God had once again wandered
from His protection by doing what was evil in His sight, and
their land was being ruined by the huge, nomadic nation of
Midian. Their altar to Baal was the central focus of their
apostasy, and even being overrun by Midian had not brought
about the repentance that was necessary. And so, all of Israel
became overwhelmed by fear as their crops were destroyed,
their livestock plundered, their children left without food. At

the point Gideon is brought to our attention, it had become common for people to make their homes in the caves of the mountains rather than on the plain, which was the natural environment needed for their usual agrarian lifestyle. Caves provided a place of refuge and a place to hide away.

Gideon, too, is afraid. And he, too, has chosen an odd place to perform normal tasks. He is threshing wheat—but doing so in a winepress. When grain was threshed, it generally was a community affair undertaken on a dedicated threshing floor, where a gathered harvest of wheat was poured out to be walked upon by animals, causing the various parts of the grain to separate. Then, the threshers would lift large scoops of crushed grain high in the air and pour them out, allowing the wind to blow the lighter "chaff" (the outside of the grains) and straw away.

Rather than do this, however, Gideon threshes alone. He has taken his wheat somewhere he hopes he won't be seen. A winepress would traditionally be a sort of pit often lined with stone or plaster, dug out in the center of a vineyard to be convenient to the newly harvested grapes for pressing.

There is all sorts of figurative language here, but it is enough to say that Gideon has changed the way he lives his life out of an abundance of well-warranted fear. The knowledge that his nation has turned its back on God and thereby been handed over to this marauding nation for punishment must have brought on a sense of dread of both God and the Midianites.

The only way Gideon could function was in hiding.

The only way Gideon could function was in hiding. And yet, notably, even here, the angel of the Lord finds him.

Gideon is full of questions, and he voices what so many of us feel when we are in a time of trial, difficulty, and fear: *If the Lord is with me, why is everything going so badly? Why isn't He doing anything about it? Obviously He has left me to fend for myself here.* The angel's response is amazing, almost comical: "Go in this your strength." Gideon's thoughts continued along the same lines: *You mean, the strength that has me hiding in a winepress? I'm the least important person in my family!* God is about to deliver the entire nation through this cowering man, and his fear has him arguing about it.

Of course, there are a myriad of stories about fear in the Word. We find Sarah afraid after the angel hears her laughing over his declaration that she and Abraham will have a son; Isaac scared the king of the Philistines will kill him in order to take his beautiful wife; Jacob terrified to meet with his brother, Esau, whom he swindled out of his birthright years before; Moses fearful when confronted with the call to lead the Israelite slaves out of captivity; the Israelites frightened when caught between the Red Sea and the oncoming Egyptian army; Joshua afraid as he is about to lead his people into the promised land . . . the examples go on and on.

Fear Sometimes Comes as a Surprising Result of Our Calling

The insistent pounding caused me to gasp as I bolted upright in bed. A quick glance at the clock told me it was 2:00 a.m., yet someone was beating at the door until it rattled in its frame. Terrified, Gwen and I clung to each other's hands in her bedroom in our little fourth-floor apartment in

Poland. We had been in Krakow only a few months, living clandestinely during the communist regime as students at the local university, avoiding our neighbors out of necessity as we met with others who wanted to learn more about God. We had memorized addresses and phone numbers in order not to carry anything bearing identification that could be traced as we traveled around the city and nearby to teach Bible studies and do our best to encourage those who were living under the control of a hostile communist government.

We weren't the only people in Krakow with secrets, of course. It was a time of little food, lots of fear, and much to learn as missionaries serving there in defiance of a government that forbade Christianity. Our apartment served as a warm haven of comfort for us as well as for those who would come to visit. While we sometimes groaned at having to carry luggage, books, and groceries up the many flights of stairs, we were grateful for the peaceful spot we'd created. The apartment itself had a secret: one wall was covered with bookshelves, and if you pushed on one of them, it opened to an otherwise unseen room just large enough for two small beds. We even had the opportunity to hide people there who would have been in danger if they had been discovered—but no one was there on this night except us.

As we sat there in fear that night, we weren't sure if our haven's door would hold. The lock got looser and looser as the men continued to assail the door, yelling threats to us. There was no way to tell who exactly it was—military police, soldiers, or angry local officials of some sort. We just knew, from others who had been hauled off to the secret police, that we should never open our door to strangers. When the pounding failed to produce the desired response, they quieted down. We looked at each other, not daring to speak. Would they leave? And then, we heard whispers. "Is that you, Sally? Pretty girl . . . come talk to us . . ." We were terrified, not knowing if they were going to make it through the door or what would happen if they did. And how did they know my name? We prayed and sang hymns quietly all night as they alternately pounded and yelled and then spoke to us in what they must have thought was an enticing way.

Body-shaking fear was real to me that night for the first time.

Our knees were knocking uncontrollably as we asked God to protect us. After several hours, they finally left, and we collapsed into some semblance of restless sleep. When we finally dared to leave the apartment later the next day, we would find our vehicle had been broken into, the door jammed; this is probably how they'd found our

Body-shaking fear was real to me that night for the first time.

information by looking in the glove compartment. Thankfully, they never returned.

Fear, however, would find other ways to threaten me over the years. Before we left Poland, we would experience rumors of war as tanks drove down main streets nearby, a bad snowstorm leading to a car accident, and being questioned by secret police. In later years, I would face several miscarriages, severe illnesses suffered by my children, a house fire, and multiple other circumstances that filled me with feelings of anxiety and dread.

Mary Felt Fear, Too

It's a scene that makes for a dramatic, sentimental picture: a lovely young girl is approached by an angel and told she is to become the mother of Jesus, the Son of God. In fine art pieces, she's usually pictured in some beautiful location: at a well, in a garden, sitting in some inexplicably Grecian bedroom (obviously not done for realism!) dressed in beautiful clothing, her face serene and accepting. The Scripture gives us a different view, though . . .

> In the sixth month of Elizabeth's pregnancy, God sent the angel Gabriel to Nazareth, a town in Galilee, to a virgin pledged to be married to a man named Joseph, a descendant of David. The virgin's name was Mary. The angel went to her and said, "Greetings, you who are highly favored! The Lord is with you."
>
> Mary *was greatly troubled at his words* and wondered what kind of greeting this might be. But the angel said to her, "Do not be afraid, Mary; you have found favor with God. You will conceive and give birth to a son, and you are to call him Jesus. He will be great and will be called the Son of the Most High. The Lord God will give him the throne of his father David, and he will reign over Jacob's descendants forever; his kingdom will never end."
>
> "How will this be," Mary asked the angel, "since I am a virgin?"
>
> Luke 1:26–34 NIV, emphasis mine

Did you catch it? *She wasn't serene at first.* When this angel appeared to Mary with such an astounding announcement, she was pledged to be married but still a virgin, living in a culture where shame and honor were tantamount, and she had just been told she would be an unwed mother. The appearance of the angel alone was probably enough to strike fear into her heart, even before he said anything at all!

It is no wonder the Bible tells us she was "greatly troubled." Mary's fear could have come from so many sources: of what her parents, Joseph, and her friends would say when they heard this incredible news; of the practical unknown matters of pregnancy, labor, and birth; of becoming the mother of the Son of God. If you've ever felt overwhelmed by the task you be-

If you've ever felt overwhelmed by the task you believe God has given to you, just remember the one He gave to Mary that day in Nazareth.

lieve God has given to you, just remember the one He gave to Mary that day in Nazareth. And yet, in the end, she said, "I am the Lord's servant. . . . May your word to me be fulfilled" (Luke 1:38 NIV). She acquiesced to God by faith and lived to serve His will.

Fear Sometimes Comes from Our Circumstances

Paul was a prisoner, bound on a ship headed to Rome. Acts 27:10 says, "Men, I can see that our voyage is going to be disastrous and bring great loss to ship and cargo, and to our own lives also" (NIV).

Paul was in the midst of a disastrous situation, and he made sure to warn his crew about the storm that he believed would cause absolute destruction. This would be a very different story if Paul left things off right there with warnings, worry, and hopelessness. However, an angel spoke to Paul and he went on to tell his crew in verse 25: "Keep up your courage, men, for I have faith in God that it will happen just as he told me" (NIV). Paul's words of hope and faith restored the crew and gave them courage.

Jesus himself encountered many disastrous situations. However, even in the midst of raging seas, He spoke peace and calm over the chaos.

How would you react if a crazy, angry, hateful crowd came up to you and attempted to throw you off a cliff? When that happened to Jesus, He simply passed through those people and went to the next town. Even when the devil plotted hate and harm against Him, Jesus never allowed anything to stand in the way of His purpose.

The coming of Jesus took away any power the enemy could have to hurt us. However, we still have to choose faith, choose courage, and choose to keep walking through the disasters until we find joy. Perhaps you are in the midst of a battle right now, a war that is raging in your heart and soul.

> *The coming of Jesus took away any power the enemy could have to hurt us.*

I challenge you to walk with courage and faith through this season, no matter how disastrous the voyage may appear to be. Just like the apostle Paul, your words of hope and faith will give you, and others, the strength and courage to keep going.

Life offers us many opportunities to become fearful. Our own sin, the attacks of others, fear of our calling, fear from natural disasters . . . all are common. I wonder if it seems to every generation that their own time has more of those fears than any before have faced. Yet because of these circumstances, this very season we live in could, from God's perspective on history, be one of the finest hours for Christians to stay true, to be faithful, to endure hardship, to rejoice in His reality, and to live by faith, "the assurance of things hoped for, the conviction of things not seen" (Hebrews 11:1 ESV).

Perhaps He has chosen us for this time in history as a trust because He knew we would be capable to be steadfast and faithful in these times. He wants us to live in Him, to allow Him to be our stability and to take away our fear. We can fight fear and anxiety by making wise choices when they overtake us, as they inevitably will. When we live in fear, we make bad decisions.

After years of learning to intentionally reject fear, I'd rather be a risk taker and live by faith, believing that God is here and listening, than to let fear stop me. I don't want fear of what might happen, fear of failure, or fear of what people might think to squeeze the life and childlikeness of believing and hoping right out of me, causing me to do nothing at all. I do not want to be the one who hid what I had in the ground, and find a frown on His face when I meet Him because I was afraid to do anything. I want to be one who invested what He has given me to please my master (Matthew 25:14–30).

We only have this day to live a faithful story. Fear should not determine how we will live. But living by faith, beyond fear, is a service of worship to Him who will bear us through.

An Anchoring
PRAYER

Heavenly Father,

Sometimes my heart becomes fearful. I know I can always ask for forgiveness if I am wrong, or admit that I am fallible, but there are some situations I just cannot control. Lord, I believe in you even though I cannot see. I trust you even though I don't understand. I am your girl. I will bring your light into dark places. I know you are here with me and I know that even though I am weak, you are always with me and you will always redeem. I know life will have its frightening aspects. Please help me build my life on trust in you and in your final authority over my life. I know you are always good to me. Help me sense your nearness today as I trust you to help me make it through the storms. In Jesus' precious name, Amen.

An Anchoring
SCRIPTURE

May our hearts be as David's, who wrote:

> The LORD is my light and my salvation;
> Whom should I fear?

The LORD is the defense of my life;
Whom should I dread?
When evildoers came upon me to devour my flesh,
My adversaries and my enemies, they stumbled
    and fell.
If an army encamps against me,
My heart will not fear;
If war arises against me,
In spite of this I am confident.

PSALM 27:1–3

When you look back over your life, where do you go for help first in times of fear?

Are there any evildoers, adversaries, or enemies in your life right now? Name them, and ask the Lord to give you courage as He steps in as your defender.

What might it look like for you to look to the Lord as your light, as well as the defense of your life?

An Anchoring
ACT

Today, as an act of your will, write out just where you need courage, and how you will take the strength of God and write a story of His miraculous grace in the midst of your fears.

SEVEN

Disappointment in Marriage

Overcoming and moving forward

With all humility and gentleness, with patience, bearing with one another in love, eager to maintain the unity of the Spirit in the bond of peace.

Ephesians 4:2–3 ESV

Fix your course on a star and you'll navigate any storm.

Leonardo da Vinci

Darkness had filled our little house in Oxford for hours, with the sun setting at 4:05. As per usual, at 6:00 sharp, we watched a bit of American news to find out just how crazy and challenging it was in our home country. It didn't take much for us to turn off the television.

Around 6:30, my homemade chicken soup with a fresh piece of toast and applesauce was the menu of choice, as I made it at least once a week. I knew Clay, my husband, would enjoy this, as his appetites are very particular, and I have learned to cook to his liking as a way I can subtly say, "You matter," to my introverted man.

We ate at the dinner table, as we almost always do. Again, my husband prefers that. And then, as he does every night, he washed the dishes and made things spotless in his meticulous way. We continued our rituals, each going our own way to wrap up the day in whatever way necessary, making phone calls to the kids or sending a stray email here and there. Next, an hour of a TV series we had been watching. Me off to a hot bath or to read in bed. and hours later Clay came upstairs after I was fast asleep at 10 or 11.

It wasn't a particularly romantic or exciting evening like the kind I dreamed of when we got engaged. There were times in my life when that kind of end to my day would have disappointed me. But it was our comfortable rhythm, developed over years, the set of habits we had adopted to give order to our lives. And the older I got, the more I realized that the comfort and security of having shaped our own patterns together gave me the great stability that I needed. Living internationally away from America meant that our rhythms developed over many years gave us life during the lockdown of the pandemic in the UK. We had partnered through every season of marriage for forty years. There was a security and stability to the life we had built together that I wouldn't trade for anything. I just didn't know that is what

I would want even more than some kind of arbitrary expectation of romantic perfection. I have lived through enough seasons to better understand what God had in mind from the beginning. He did not have a Hollywood movie, with perfect sexual pleasure, deeply thoughtful and sensitive romance, a perfect life and home in mind when He designed marriage and companionship for men and women.

All marriages are different, have strengths and weaknesses, and are a covenant between people with differing personalities, maturity, and skills. And the reality is that some marriages are more satisfying than others and some people are more compatible in a moment-by-moment review. There is no one type of marriage that fits all. But growth in wisdom, maturity, and experience leads us to understand what a partnership in life is all about. It takes time to have a golden marriage.

In Genesis 2:18, God said, "It is not good for the man to be alone; I will make him a helper suitable for him." At the very beginning, marriage was about partnership, companionship so that neither would have to face the storms of life alone. Man and woman were given to each other to create life and build a legacy of faith and faithfulness. It took me some years to understand the very heart of marriage as something not out of a romance novel, but for my own good, for stability, for help, for growth.

Deep disappointment in marriage, lack of intimacy and romance, isolation and loneliness come to most women in the winter seasons of their marriage. Storms of relationship discord come and go between imperfect people. But wisdom brings healing and depth that grows over a lifetime. Just as wisdom in parenting grows over time, understanding of life and perspective on what matters develops over years, so the value of a seasoned and blessed marriage takes time and patience.

These sorts of commitments and details are not popular to our cultural expectations. We want results and fulfillment now, not later. The details of how to grow in a fulfilling marriage would require another long book, but I hope the principles I have communicated here might encourage you to keep going and keep growing through the storms to find ultimate deep soul satisfaction.

Serving God in Marriage

I have shared a story many times about an evening when I was at my wits' end over a strong disagreement we had. I was lying in bed, tears running down, and in a sense shaking my fist at God. I was, of course, rehearsing my rights, my sense of justice, assuming that my way of seeing our circumstances was right. I told God how hard it had been and what I expected. Then, as I waited in the quiet, God's voice came through.

What if the only thing I ever wanted you to do for my sake was to love Clay unconditionally? What if you are the vehicle through which he will receive unconditional love and respect as a human being? What if you are the agent I chose to show him what commitment and respect are like? You said you would follow me, serve me. If this is what I wanted you to do, even if no one else knew your sacrifice, would you do that for me?

> *What if the only thing I ever wanted you to do for my sake was to love Clay unconditionally?*

The only answer I could give was, "Yes, for you I will do anything. You are my Lord."

Until that moment, I had not fully realized that my faithfulness and choice to grow in unselfishness was not as much for Clay as it was for God. Everything in my life was an issue of worshipping Him in that place, in those circumstances. My marriage and my motherhood, in so many ways, even with endless life-storms, were a training ground for my walk with God.

And so, every year, we strained toward understanding, seeking to be partners in this work of life, both having to give up a lot. So many times, I thought I was giving up more than he was. But I learned that straining to see Clay in context, to learn to accept the limitations of his personality, gave me a way to become more of a peacemaker, to grow in gentleness and the kind of love God had for me.

Finally, after years, we began to see that one of the best gifts we ever gave to our children was to stay married, to work toward unconditional love again and again. And now we see that in a world that doesn't believe in faithful, committed love, it was one of the best gifts we could give as a legacy to our children, so that they, too, could learn to be servant marriage partners. And in the midst of it all, our marriage became a treasure, a place of deep satisfaction, because we had learned the value of unconditional love and respect. When we began, it was just a theological idea. After forty years, we knew it to be sacred, a secret about the long-suffering of God with us less-than-perfect children.

Marriage is a foundational stronghold for building culture. Marriage is the first community where two people come together to manifest mutual partnership in bringing God's reality, beauty, and truth to the world. And marriage sets up a place for family, home, faith, and heritage to grow.

All marriages are populated with sinful, immature, imperfect, self-absorbed people with extremely differing personalities. All of us fall short. All of us have to learn to give in.

I'm not talking about blind submission. Clay has had to put up with a lot, waiting for me to grow up and to learn how to be a companion more responsive to his needs and desires. Learning better how to serve him as a worthy friend and lover, for the sake of Christ, has been a long, hard journey. But now we have this treasure of a legacy of faithful love and a godly heritage.

We would never be able to identify with those in the arena of our influence if our lives had been ideal and we were perfectly matched and had never struggled through the storms. But it is in making it through the storms, which at times seemed impossible, that the value of our many years grew with each anniversary. It is through humility and failing and finding mercy and grace from Him that we can now serve others who are coming behind us.

I want to acknowledge that I have many friends who gave and sacrificed, and still they ended up with a broken marriage and are now single parents. And yet they are able to model love to their children in a broken world swirling with storms. And God still is there to guide, lead, love, heal. Life is complex.

Needed: A Clear Vision

Starting out with a proper vision helps determine the success of any great venture. Long after the sparkle and expectations of romance in marriage have worn off, the vision of what marriage means will be the glue holding that union together.

Marriage was created to be a foundation for all of life. God created Adam and Eve, together, to be the unit through which the world would become organized, the first community group. In this union, God intended that we find stability, comfort, and meaning. The family was the structure through which purpose would be given and comfort in companionship experienced, life celebrated and traditions kept, and grace given with love and mutual respect. It was also the place where righteousness would be passed down from generation to generation. As the family goes, so goes the culture, the nation. What a person does to build her marriage and family might be the greatest, most long-lasting work of her life.

Long after the sparkle and expectations of romance in marriage have worn off, the vision of what marriage means will be the glue holding that union together.

Each wedding, then, inaugurates a potentially beautiful new story of heritage, love, faithful living, and historic impact. *What will this couple do for the kingdom of God? How will they influence nations, institutions, neighborhoods?* There are myriads of generations potentially down the line who will build upon this same foundation as they craft homes of their own.

It is up to us what sort of foundation those generations will build upon. Marriage is where we have the opportunity to live out faithfulness, regardless of the difficulties we face.

Of course, there are many tragic stories of unfaithfulness, abuse, and breaking of covenant, and God's grace is powerful to comfort and help those who find themselves in such circumstances. He is able to redeem and restore and help us when we are in desperate need. I have seen His grace and life-giving redemption work in miraculous ways to bring restoration to people broken because of the destruction of marriage so rampant in today's world.

I do want to speak here, though, to those who are still married. To be a good wife is not simple, nor does it come naturally and easily to me or to almost any woman. It calls upon all the best I can possibly be in my thoughts, actions, creativity, prayer life, and the way I bring beauty into the day by day. It seems that in this self-centered time, we often focus on whether our husband is or is not fulfilling what we see as our needs. Yet marriage must truly become more about pleasing God than pleasing ourselves. His wisdom that led me forward was the road to growing in a personal understanding of the unchangeable love of Christ for me, with all of my imperfections. The lessons I learned hammered my heart to make me more sympathetic to others in their needs, more compassionate in situations that required the mercy and kindness of God. Marriage is a sanctifying road that has helped me to access my best self that had never been developed before.

I think when we consider this most difficult and close-to-the-heart relationship, the best place to start is not with behavior (*Have you kept the law of marriage?*) but with the heart. What is truly in your heart as it relates to your husband? "She does him good and not evil all the days of her life," Proverbs 31:12 says. What does it mean to do my husband good? I think it means the Lord wants my heart to be soft, flexible in responding to my husband, being aware of his weaknesses and strengths. I need to consider . . . *How can I be a friend and companion to him? Enjoy him? Encourage him? Honor him? What is my attitude toward God, in light of how I behave in my marriage?* As I act this out, my children learn about unconditional love, friendship, marriage, life.

Having a vision is a good place to begin, and it's never too late to determine what your own vision will be. You may have come to know the Lord after you married, and so you did not begin with these things in mind. As time goes on and the reality of marriage begins to set in, it's important to determine that we will love and respect our husbands in order to please God because that is our commitment. That vow comes before our vows to all others—including ourselves. If I consider everything I do, even marriage, as a way to worship God, I can find grace and hope to get through difficult times.

> *If I consider everything I do, even marriage, as a way to worship God, I can find grace and hope to get through difficult times.*

Often, we think we know what will fulfill us, and just as often, it may not be the spouse in front of you. But for me, learning to love more deeply, and learning to "put up with" is a two-way street. Stretching toward my capacity to be steadfast has left me with a more grateful heart and an understanding that God's ways do lead to deeper, long-term satisfaction. Self-centered, self-absorbed decisions often lead to emptiness.

Five Principles to Help Weather the Storms of Marriage

Do unto your husband as you would have him do unto you.

We are all familiar with the golden rule, and many think of it primarily as a good thing to teach our children or to live out with our neighbors. Yet I wonder, sometimes, if we don't consider ourselves exempt from following it! Taking time to consider our own desires, and then realizing that our husbands are people, too (surprise!) and have those same needs—for respect, consideration, and kindness—can go a long way as we strive to build marriages worth living in, and worth passing on.

> *Each time we wound our husbands we are also wounding ourselves.*

If your parents didn't give you a model of this kind of marriage, and those around you aren't living out this kind of relationship (which is true for so many of us), you may find yourself acting out old patterns of bitterness, a short temper, selfishness, and gossip. Yet we have to remember that since we have become "one flesh" (Genesis 2:24), each time we wound our husbands we are also wounding ourselves. We exacerbate our own pain by inflicting it on our spouse. You may feel changing is too hard or hopeless, or find yourself making excuses—"This is just the way I've been and it's all I know." Yet I am sure your heart wants more than this for your home, and so does the Lord. He is near to help; just ask.

Seek to understand.

We all need grace, understanding, and allowance for growth, and that goes for husbands, too. This idea, to seek to understand even before being understood, originated in the Prayer of St. Francis. Its earliest-known publication in 1912 is translated thus:

> Lord, make me an instrument of your peace.
> Where there is hatred, let me bring love.
> Where there is offense, let me bring pardon.
> Where there is discord, let me bring union.
> Where there is error, let me bring truth.
> Where there is doubt, let me bring faith.
> Where there is despair, let me bring hope.
> Where there is darkness, let me bring your light.
> Where there is sadness, let me bring joy.
> O Master, let me not seek as much
> to be consoled as to console,
> to be understood as to understand,
> to be loved as to love,
> for it is in giving that one receives,
> it is in self-forgetting that one finds,
> it is in pardoning that one is pardoned,
> it is in dying that one is raised to eternal life.[1]

What a beautiful prayer. I think I shall write this one out myself and put it where I can read it every day to remind myself! It is such a powerful gift to offer someone the grace of understanding, and one that will be a blessing to us as we extend it to our spouses.

Clay and I think so differently, and I realize looking back that many times when we would disagree, I would judge his motives. Yet, now, I try to see behind the words to understand his personality and *why he said what he did*. I have also taken to heart Jesus' admonition to be a peacemaker

(Matthew 5:9). I have learned that making and giving peace is often more important than my need to be right. And the older I get, the more I see that disagreeing over small and insignificant differences of opinion is draining and a waste of my time and energy. It is so much more pleasant to do the work of getting along.

Don't make your husband an idol; he cannot fill all of your needs and was never supposed to.

Being put on a pedestal sounds like a nice idea, and I do hear from many women who have idolized their husbands or even the idea of marriage. Perhaps they came from unhappy homes, and just know things will be perfect when they have a home of their own. Sometimes it happens when a woman's parents do have a happy marriage, and she assumes her own will be just the same. Yet behind these ideals is reality, which means a lot of work! Because we are all sinful, regular humans who get tired and cranky, sick and worried, older and slower, and generally face ups and downs, our husbands will not always match our vision of Mr. Right.

A friend once told me she'd had a discussion with her husband in which she was sharing a mutual friend's desperation for her husband's absolute attention at all times. Her husband surprised her when he said, *There's a lot to be said for being your own person!* "You know, I love it that you have your own life. You have your own friends, and you work and reach out to other moms. You teach our children and others' and have ministry things you do at church. I like it that you're a person in your own right. It takes the pressure off of me to be everything." There's a lot to be said for being your own person!

Pressure to live up to perfection is no fun, as it causes one to feel entirely responsible for someone else's entertainment, emotional stability, and affection. Give your husband a break in this area—be your own person, and invite other people to be part of your life!

Seek to serve in order to worship God.

> An excellent wife who can find?
>   She is far more precious than jewels.
> The heart of her husband trusts in her,
>   and he will have no lack of gain.
> She does him good, and not harm,
>   all the days of her life.
>
> Proverbs 31:10–12 ESV

> To the extent that you did it for one of the least of these brothers or sisters of Mine, you did it for Me.
>
> Matthew 25:40

One very important thing I have learned over these many years, as I've shared here, is that service to my husband (or children or friend or neighbor)—whether helping him solve a dilemma, praying for him, washing his laundry, or organizing a family vacation—is actually a service to the Lord. The Bible makes it clear we are called to serve one another, care for one another, and put others before ourselves. This certainly holds true for the way we are to interact with our husbands. Jesus also says that whatever we do for others, we have actually done for Him. Looking at my daily, often mundane work this way puts it in a different light, lending a sense of honor to the simplest efforts. Rather than resenting my to-do list, reminding myself that I am doing each task for the Lord has a way of changing my attitude and helping me serve with gladness.

I am a very independent woman. I travel; I have my own profession. I cherish my own opinions, and I like the freedom to live and determine a lot of my own schedule. But I have also found that humbly serving and delighting in my children and husband out of my own choice has given me the best friends and closest community I could ever imagine. It is not out of some legalistic, patriarchal command that I give of myself. It is out of following hard after the model of Christ and finding it to be freeing and deeply satisfying after all these years.

Have the end in mind; think of your grandchildren and those you'll influence.

We live in a fast-paced society that values speed, efficiency, and accomplishment. Most of us live by the dictates of our planners and goal-setting schemes, and there's much to be said for having schedules, routines, and vision, which help direct the way we spend our time. Yet when it comes to marriage, this sort of results-driven mentality can work against us because it tends to focus on results that are short-term. We say, "Ahhh, this is what I've accomplished _____" with "today/this week/this month/this year" in the blank. Even long-term goal setting tends to be in terms of having a five-year plan.

But we must look at marriage with an eye to the future. I'm talking more of a fifty-year plan. Wrapping our minds around that kind of commitment, that kind of longevity (read: long-suffering and perseverance) is very outside our normal, practiced planning muscles. That kind of thinking is God-thinking. Only He could have come up with the idea that two people would commit to stay together, forsaking all others, for the purpose of building a family and having children and passing on faith and love for generations. No one else would have thought it possible!

When Clay and I look back over the years, we can see that through a boatload of hard work, faithfulness, and growing, we have left a legacy for our children: many books carved out of the story of our lives, a ministry that has spanned decades, and a faith that led

> *We must look at marriage with an eye to the future—a fifty-year plan.*

us, through thick and thin, to leave a picture of what God's grace looks like when two individuals give up their lives to build something together that is more worthwhile than either life would have been alone.

Becoming a grandmother has been such a surprising, precious gift to me. To look across the room and see my husband cradling our new grandson, looking into his wondering blue eyes, smiling down at this third generation—it is nothing but a testimony of grace that brings me so much joy. It allows me to see the "why" of the many long years of *staying the course.*

Not all marriages are blessed with natural children, of course. Not all will marry. I believe, though, that this grandparent-grace-feeling is very akin to the emotion I experience when Clay and I meet with people we have had the honor of ministering to over the course of many years, after we haven't seen them for a long time. To sit there, the two of us still together, still offering our friendship and whatever it is we might be able to offer in wisdom and encouragement to a single person, a church, or another couple feels miraculous. *Because it is.* A long-range vision has been a deeply necessary foundation to our lives. We want to be able to look back and say, "Our faithfulness has been worth it; look at all this fruit!"

Looking Ahead

At the close of this chapter, let me just say I realize we live in a broken world, and for some, life has brought a story you never expected. Perhaps there is no opportunity left for you to work toward grace and vision in marriage, because those bonds have already been broken. Please know I am so sorry for the pain I know this must have caused. I trust the Lord will be present in your life. He loves you deeply and will be faithful to walk with you throughout all your days, regardless of your marriage status.

For others, your difficulties remain, right alongside your marriage vows. Our God is a God of redemption, and thankfully He can restore and heal the wounds that too often come from anger, harshness, and unfaithfulness in marriage. I have also seen that when one spouse is mature and behaves honorably before children, even in broken, difficult marriages, the children can still be healthy and strong and led to emotional maturity because they have seen grace in the face of foul play, and gentleness in the face of selfishness from one parent. The hope we have in Jesus and His ability to answer prayer and to redeem is beyond our comprehension.

God is ready to help and draw near to us as we set our hearts toward finding peace, grace, and hope in our marriages, bringing light to our days as well as the lives of those around us. May we all reach toward Him as our constant source of grace and hope, especially in this tender area, and stay fast in the midst of our marriage storms.

Finally, throw caution to the wind. Kiss your husband passionately, laugh at his humor, enter into his music, don't get caught in petty arguments, and celebrate the life you have. Life is short. This is your stage, where joy can be cultivated.

An Anchoring
PRAYER

Dearest Lord,

I am so glad you are here as part of my marriage. Please help me remember the promises we made to one another and to You. Please remind me of the things I loved about my spouse when we were dating, and of all the things that are still so good about him. Help me remember that I am imperfect, too, and that you are always so patient with me. Let me keep the goal of pleasing you first in my heart. Strengthen me to remain faithful and kind, and help me love as you do. In Jesus' precious name, Amen.

An Anchoring
SCRIPTURE

Love is patient, love is kind, it is not jealous; love does not brag, it is not arrogant. It does not act disgracefully, it does not seek its own benefit; it is not provoked, does not keep an account of a wrong suffered, it does not rejoice in unrighteousness, but rejoices with the truth; it keeps every confidence, it believes all things, hopes all things, endures all things.

1 CORINTHIANS 13:4–7

This passage is read so often at weddings, yet I wonder if we think of it as we experience difficulties with our spouses.

When we rehearse their mistakes, are we being patient?

When we push for our way, are we being kind?

When we are suspicious of the way they spend their time, are we being jealous?

Spend some time with this Scripture, asking God to show you your own heart. Write down your reflections below.

An Anchoring
ACT

Make a meal or teatime date with your husband. The point of this exercise is to have some time alone to talk. Ask him questions about his life, his childhood, his perspective on how he feels about his job, children, life as it is now. Don't be defensive. Determine to see his heart and his deep desires. Grow in understanding why your husband sees life as he does. Extend grace, verbal appreciation, and affirmation as an exercise of kindness to him. Hopefully, this practice will help you to grow closer over years. Journal about what you learn about him below.

EIGHT

Unexpected Challenges with Our Children

Love is key

Above all, keep fervent in your love for one another, because love covers a multitude of sins.

1 Peter 4:8

Can the boat sink while Thou, dear Lord, are in it?

Amy Carmichael, *Toward Jerusalem*

Whenen I discovered I was pregnant at thirty years old, I knew nothing of babies or children. I had babysat less than a handful of times in my life, and as the only girl in my three-child family, I had never

152

really taken to baby dolls. As a teen, I dreamed of romance but never even thought about being a mama.

Consequently, when I was finally on my way to motherhood, I read every book on maternity, motherhood, and parenting I could find. After months of thinking through all these ideas, I was pretty sure I could copy what I had learned and follow the advice and systems of the authorities. I expected I would be competent, as I'd accomplished most other things I'd sent my mind to. My children would certainly be charming, darling, and delightful to me and to everyone else.

My children would certainly be charming, darling, and delightful to me and to everyone else.

Thirty-nine weeks pregnant at my baby shower, with thirty-five women celebrating my new baby, I felt a growing sense of confidence and ease. "You've got this!" "You will be a natural!" (Whatever that means!) Since I had the Bradley Method of childbirth memorized, I just knew I would sail through the next few weeks. I was almost thirty-one years old and I am not sure I had even held a baby, but I had read books!

As I walked down the hallway at the end of the baby shower, I ran into a woman I did not know well. I can still see her face in my mind today. She looked determined, and emotionally fraught. "Don't you believe all of those women," she said, as she grabbed hold of my arm. "This is not going to be easy. Birthing the baby will hurt more than you could ever imagine. You will be exhausted from getting no sleep for months on end, and you will struggle to figure out how to train and control your babies. Prepare yourself, girlfriend! Motherhood is no picnic."

I thought to myself, *Wow, she's a bit rude and abrasive. What a negative person. Too bad she goes through life with such a negative outlook!*

Motherhood Is No Picnic

And then, I had Sarah. She ended up in the ICU unable to breathe after twenty-three hours of heavy labor . . . and that, my friends, is all I have time to tell you about her. Suffice it to say, her entry into the world was challenging and stretching, and it left me feeling confused.

Years later, I found myself with three babies aged four and under, all ear-infected most of the time and asthmatic, as I had been as a baby. On one particularly rough day, I recalled the lady who had tried to warn me at the shower so long before, and I mused, "She's the only one who had the confidence to tell me the truth about motherhood. This is soooo hard."

Storms come at regular intervals and with gale-force winds when we enter the gigantic and auspicious task of bringing real human beings into the world and shepherding them to adulthood. I find it interesting that one of the most profoundly shaping stewardships of human beings comes with almost no universal truths or training in most of our culture. We enter these overwhelming life-storms unprepared and untrained, and yet the outcome has huge consequences.

My first two children did provide big changes to my life, and I did have to stretch to figure out motherhood, but I was gently getting the hang of it little by little. What I did not know then was that these two, who had turned my life upside down, were my easy children!

Nathan, my third, had one easy day when he was born. (I remember, because it was also the day Joel screamed all day because he'd had ear surgery.) But after that first day, little Nathan screamed and cried much of the day, staying awake hours upon hours, and though he ate, he was not always comforted by nursing. By eighteen months, he was having multiple loud meltdowns every day. Nathan may have had stomach issues. But as I look back, I think he had clinical OCD—and a very strong personality—even as a little baby. Handling the three of them while Clay worked a mandatory seventy hours a week left me gasping for help and answers.

I have received hundreds of letters or messages from well-intentioned mothers who are totally fraught with the daily storms of conflict in their homes because of a challenging child with emotional, personality, relational, or behavioral issues. Children turn the worlds of parents upside down, and the storms of dealing with such life-turbulence seem never ending.

Children turn the worlds of parents upside down, and the storms of dealing with such life-turbulence seem never ending.

The stories of my life people identify with most have been the Nathan stories. Maybe it was because Nathan stories always included how often he challenged me, screamed and cried as a little one, resisted sleep, and was not generally compliant as a little boy. That sweet boy (who towers over me now) was the source of so much angst and joy all at the same time! I learned so much about the love of my own heavenly Father as I walked as a mama to Nathan. When Nathan and I wrote *Different:*

The Story of an Outside-the-Box Kid and the Mom Who Loved Him together, it helped me know both of them even better.

Many people have said to me, "I have a Nathan, too!" I think they usually mean they have a child who always makes them push a little harder than they ever expected as a parent! Some children are just naturally more gregarious and active, or perhaps extremely timid and afraid. Some have truly diagnosis-worthy differences. So many mamas feel the stress of having children who just don't fit in the box, or don't easily sync into the parent's personality preferences. Perhaps they are too loud, don't potty train when expected, don't sleep through the night even when everything has been tried. Then, as they grow, many exhibit unusual behavior, which often leads to a diagnosis of some sort, whether right or wrong. I know now that some of these irregularities are pretty normal, and that many children will grow out of the challenges and into healthy adults. Yet, children come with a personality and immaturity at the same time. This means it will take time to fully access their potential. To find stability in these relational storms, we need to see forward to the possibility of what they will grow into and believe in who they are becoming a little at a time.

None of my children are the same. Three out of four have mental illness (clinical OCD and a couple of other issues). I have mental illness in my greater family (bipolar disorder and OCD). Yet I found that none of my friends wanted to talk to me about it. They just wanted to pretend my children were normal. (Is there such a thing as a normal child, when every child has a different DNA, different fingerprints, differing personalities?)

All of Us Are Different

I've come to realize over the years that all of us are different, in some way. And all of us are flawed and imperfect as a result of being born in this world. Of course, because of our own personalities, our children can drive us crazy if they are very different than us—or they at least push our buttons on a regular basis! Some of these differences are personality driven, and sometimes they are issue or emotion driven. And sometimes these screaming little ones are acting out of exhaustion, hunger, overstimulation, or neglect. But I learned with Nathan that some of his differences actually were a reflection of the role God had called him to in his life.

Some of his differences actually were a reflection of the role God had called him to in his life.

Nathan is a debater who cares deeply about truth and is unabashedly bold in helping others, sharing his life and goods with down-and-out people. As an immature little boy, his arguing felt like disrespect, but I learned to understand that he was learning to argue as practice for eventually representing justice and righteousness in his greater world. So, of course, I wish I had understood more about his heart and not judged him through so many little-boy days.

Nathan writes:

> I've always known I was different. It wasn't something I chose or an identity I one day decided to wear. Being different is woven into the very fabric of who I am. Part of it comes from the various "disorders" that have challenged me and my

family, and part of it simply comes from the outside-the-box personality God decided to give me.

Being different has made itself evident in every corner of my life, peeking out and reminding me whenever I start to think I might be normal.

I know I'm different because when other children were content with walking on the sidewalk, I felt the need to climb the rails. Because when others' questions would stop, mine seemed to go on without end, often frustrating those who ran out of answers.

I know I'm different because when I was fifteen I began taking six showers a day and washing my hands until they bled.

I know I'm different because my mind seems to change channels at will, making it nearly impossible to focus on any one thing for more than a few minutes.

I know I'm different because no matter how hard I looked at the math problem or how many times my tutor explained it, my mind simply couldn't grasp the simple numerical basics that seemed to come so easy to my friends and siblings.

I know I'm different because while I long for affection, I am often scared to touch the ones I love for fear of contaminating them. . . .

I know I'm different because I've been told so by every important person in my life.[1]

There are an infinite number of ways to be different and to feel like one doesn't fit in. What if every child—your child—is hiding feelings like this inside? Wouldn't you want to understand and sympathize? Nathan's case, it turned out, did involve several clinical disorders as well as a number of personality quirks that set him apart from the crowd. When Nathan and I began writing the story of his life in our book, *Different: The Story of an Outside-the-Box Kid and the Mom Who Loved Him,* I realized that I, too, had felt different my whole life.

I am passionate, outspoken, and engaged in ways most of my friends and acquaintances are not. Sometimes that makes me feel outside the norm. But what if God made me this way to fit me for the very ministry I have been in for most of my adult life? What if my differences have equipped me to speak to thousands, and to be driven to write messages and podcast and to blog for many years? All of us have a story to tell and a place to be faithful, and we will find it fits how we have been designed—differences and all.

Feeling different, *being* different, is something our culture, especially Christian culture, does not talk about much. People often turn their heads away from people and situations they don't understand and pretend they do not exist. The words *mental illness* can make them positively squirm. (If you'd like to read more of the story, I hope you will pick up a copy of *Different: The Story of an Outside-the-Box Kid and the Mom Who Loved Him.* Nathan came to me to propose this book so that we could help others. He and I are overwhelmed by the many messages we receive every day from people all over the world who love this book and the way it encourages them to find the foundation of love and acceptance from which to influence their children. We have found that it encourages all parents, not just those whose child seems out of the box, because all children long to be understood and loved as they are.)

Differences Are a Gift

As mothers, we have a variety of mixed feelings, good and disconcerting, about the children we have in our own families. And yet, we are committed to loving them. All of us have Achilles' heels: uniquely vulnerable areas of our bodies, minds, and personalities. And some of us, to be honest, are a little quirkier than others—which is why we struggle so much—and why other people, especially parents, teachers, and authority figures, have a hard time dealing with us. We are not "convenient" to their expectations of how life ought to play itself out. Don't take on unnecessary guilt for struggling as a mama. With each storm, we learn how to best deal with the wind and the waves that come our way.

But these personality differences, these outside-the-box preferences and approaches to life, don't have to be liabilities. Or they don't have to be only liabilities. They can actually be gifts to us and to others who are willing to look at life through our unique lenses. This verse has served me well:

> Above all, keep fervent in your love for one another, because love covers a multitude of sins.
>
> 1 Peter 4:8

The Pain of Parenting Is Like No Other

Children who make out-of-the-box decisions can cause us pain, too. Many mamas are heartbroken because after a lifetime of serving, training, and loving their precious children, those children become prodigals who leave the faith, choose an immoral lifestyle, or choose nontraditional sexual identities. Some develop addictions, or even commit suicide.

So many I have met feel outside the circle of acceptance as they deal with the discouragement and heartbreak of judgment from others. Fellow believers are supposed to be the ones who help bear our burdens, encourage us, and help us through difficult passages. And yet, often it is in the faith community where judgment, contention, and rejection are the harshest. This indeed is a life-storm that often leaves a wake of scars and emotional destruction that is hard to overcome.

To make it out of this attack of a life-storm when our children are not what we expected, we must be openhanded and openhearted to God and say, "Teach me to see the heart of my child. Help me to know I am exactly the mother this child needs. Cause me to understand that these differences are a place where I can honor you and serve my child with the love of Christ."

Gentleness Is Key as We Live with Our Different-from-Us Children

Even if our children aren't quantifiably, diagnosis-level "different," they are still different from us. No one is a carbon copy—and that would be boring anyway, right? Our children are wired with their own personalities and talents, dreams and goals, likes and dislikes. Sometimes those differences clash with our own. Yet here we are, living in the same four walls, twenty-four hours a day, seven days a week, fifty-two weeks of the year, for at least a couple of decades. What's a mama to do? Here's a key I've found that helps so much when things get difficult and tensions rise:

A gentle answer turns away wrath,
But a harsh word stirs up anger.

Proverbs 15:1

I assumed that when I became a wife and mother, I would automatically be mature, healthy, loving, and successful at these relationships. I did not understand the demands and weight of being a mother at all. Then conflict in my own heart and life and the stress of living with so many needs and so many demands showed me my selfishness in new ways. I was so disappointed in myself when I lost patience, acted in an unloving way, even resented my children. But I longed for mercy. I wanted to be understood. I wanted someone to recognize that I had a heart to be good at these relationships, but sometimes I just couldn't. I meant to be patient, giving, and loving, but I had my limits.

I learned that my children had all these same limits. It was through my children and the demands of everyday life that I learned the need for gentleness. Where does a woman find the ability to be gentle, to show mercy and understanding and compassion? I believe it comes as she understands that her heart is selfish, prone to making bad choices, limited in patience, and only just beginning to understand what love requires. Mamas long for grace and a gentle, sympathetic response from others in their lives.

It was through my children and the demands of everyday life that I learned the need for gentleness.

A mother learns and understands that she herself is fragile and needy. She then realizes that her children, too, have the same issues and needs. She will extend grace to those she loves because they, too, are fragile and want gentleness and mercy. As she reaches out to God for His mercy, she will find herself offering it to others more and more often.

Giving a soft answer is part of showing grace. When a baby is fussing, a child is arguing, or a teen is angry and lashing out, our first reaction is sometimes to rise to harshness ourselves. We want to meet force with force, because our own desires are not being acknowledged or our authority is being challenged. Sadly, often we are simply angry that our comfort is being disturbed by someone else's need. Yet meeting anger with anger is the least likely way to be helpful when will meets will. Anger usually breeds more anger. Proverbs 15:1 proves true over and over in my own life: "A gentle answer turns away wrath."

Returning strength for strength or anger for anger or impatience for impatience may be what comes naturally. But if a mama understands that her children, like her, are going to make mistakes, have accidents, and show the dark heart of sin, she will not condemn them harshly for doing so. Instead, from a heart that knows *she* does not deserve the grace and love of Jesus but receives it nonetheless, she will extend her patience and mercy and gentleness to her children to show them the real heart of Jesus. Part of straining toward maturity is showing patience, grace, mercy, love, and compassion.

Offering grace for our children's differences doesn't mean we neglect to train them, however. A mother who seeks to live in an understanding manner with her children will still teach and train and correct as Jesus did, but with the gentleness and compassion that come from a humbled heart.

Challenges at Every Stage

Mothers may find themselves disappointed because their lives feel less-than in some way. Daily life with young children can have a true sense of smallness embedded in it. As we wash and feed and clothe our little ones, there is little impressive "fruit" visible in our lives—especially if one envisions the ideal of large-scale visible professional work as the only valid work. Laundry piles high along with the dishes, and our kitchens seem to be one revolving mess after another. It can be difficult to spend most all of one's days in the company of tiny, demanding persons who cannot even talk yet! Parenting is quite a shock to those who have been used to having more power and control over their schedules, or even wearing clothes unmarred by spit-up and various other bodily fluids.

When our children enter elementary-aged years, there is definitely a shift. Now they are able to communicate, and there is such sweetness in our interactions as we walk the path of life together. Yet this time, too, can seem insignificant. Many mothers wonder, *What happened to what I wanted to do with my life? How much longer will I have to wait to focus on what I'm really interested in?* as their children continue to need them pretty exclusively. While we all have different puzzles of life and schedules, every parent is caught in the wrestling between meaningful work and being actively present as much as possible for our children. This wrestling is exacerbated by the seeming smallness of this season.

Then, the teen years are legendarily difficult for a multitude of reasons. Storms of emotions can rise at any time and seem to tear apart the peace and stability previously enjoyed. There is the typical angst that occurs as our children grow toward adulthood and have so many more opinions about the issues of life, as well as very strong feelings about the way we direct *our* own lives (and theirs). We may also be surprised by feelings of nostalgia and a longing to be back in their stage, with all of life ahead of us and different decisions still on the table as possibilities. I have often thought it unfair that my children and I went through such massive hormonal changes at the same time!

Of course, our children's eventual leaving of the nest, building their own families, and potentially moving away from where we are is a natural yet difficult part of life that can make us feel unimportant, unneeded, again! Isn't it funny how each of these stages is so different, yet each has the ability to make us feel similarly—insignificant in some way? Perhaps this is a sign that we are looking for our significance somewhere it cannot be found.

Isn't it funny how each of these stages is so different, yet each has the ability to make us feel similarly—insignificant in some way?

Parenting is a long-range task. It requires us to lay our lives down, to focus for a season on the needs of someone else. Does that sound familiar? It requires us to consider the needs of people who are unable to meet their own needs, and to seek God's wisdom about how to nurture and disciple and serve them well. If we recognize the importance and beauty of our work, we become able to move beyond our natural self-centeredness and grow in ways we could never have imagined.

The Fruit of Our Labor

One beautiful evening last summer, one of my sweet daughters and I walked our familiar evening path arm in arm, sharing hearts and finding solace in our companionship. The beauty of one more flurry of pinks and golds warmed our hearts as the sun settled in for the night. We knew we were not alone; God walked with us and smiled at us through His clouds and presence in our friendship.

Upon returning home, we lingered in the moonlight on our front porch, each of us rocking in our chair gently as we talked more of life. Eventually, the rest of the family all wound up gathered on the porch in the twilight. Comfort, belonging, peace, security, and stability were the feelings almost tangible in our little family group that evening. We belong to each other. We know the comfort singular to family bonds amongst our trials, our joys, our doubts, our happiness, and our anger.

As I glance back over the pathways of our story, there were many trials and obstacles along the way—car accidents, cancer, deaths, births, illnesses, financial problems, church splits, relationships coming to an end, new ones beginning. Yet, by God's grace, we have come to know that we have a harbor in our storms, and our family's mutual love has wrapped us further in the bonds that come from practicing and being loyal, strong, devoted, and present with one another through each day, each year, each conflict.

How did it happen? Not by accident! There were thousands of meals shared, birthday celebrations when each sibling was encouraged to share something kind about the special one, story times where we shared in rousing and touching and inspiring tales that became part of our family culture, and, of course, a lot of prayer. Family, I am convinced, was designed by God so that we could have our emotional needs met. Grandparents, aunts and uncles, cousins, parents were meant to provide help, comfort, wisdom, sharing of traditions, history, purpose, morality, and celebration through the seasons of life.

That is why the breakdown of the family is such a strategic move for Satan. If he can rob us of the support systems, accountability, encouragement, and tangible love of God that was supposed to be given through our relationships with the many people to whom we belong, then he breaks down the foundations upon which we were supposed to build righteousness and godly purpose. People tend to drift and wander when they don't have connection and responsibility of relationships to a family. We become an easy target for Satan when we isolate ourselves and are alone.

At my age, in spite of past fear that life-storms would overwhelm, I have lived to see the fingerprints of God all over our days. We loved and had fun with each other out of necessity and intention, and the end result is that we are friends who love and enjoy each other not because we have to, but because we truly are interested in one another. So I can say, even though your children fuss and argue and you get exasperated many days, if you plan shared times and experiences for your family and purpose to walk in grace as much as possible, you will be surprised years from now to find you've built real friendships, right in your own home.

You will be surprised years from now to find you've built real friendships, right in your own home.

Some take-away principles to move toward grace and hope:

1. Understand that unconditional love is at the heart of all long-lasting influence. Love is God's way of reaching and transforming people. When the winds of storms begin to thrash about in relationship to your children, keep in mind that love will be the secret that calms the raging waves. Leaving a legacy of unconditional love in the lives of our children is profoundly important to our own long-term relationship with them and in providing safe sailing ahead. My friendships with my children are the most deeply gratifying relationships I have ever had. Loving well and long is worth the investment.

2. Accept your child for who they are right now. Accept that storms and frustration are a part of all relationships. If you face storms with calm because you know they won't last forever, riding in the boat together will be a more serene experience. Don't make your love and affirmation based on their current behavior, or hold it tight and refuse to give it to them until sometime in the future when they meet your expectations. God has created them as they are for us to cherish and enjoy and appreciate right now and every day.

3. Facing a life of continual interruptions by threatening storms is emotionally difficult and wearying. Yet, a view for long-term understanding and acceptance of the storm, while asking God to bring grace, can help you to find your footing for the difficult times. Try to build breaks into your weekly schedule so you can get

away from the constant stress. Accept the fact that your child's issues, diagnosis, or difficulty may never change. There is no magic bullet. Submitting to that reality puts the burden of his or her life in the hands of God. He is responsible for moving and working, and He will give you grace for the long haul. And in the end, you will be more gracious, loving, patient, and sympathetic to all human beings. But do seek to find ways you might refresh, renew, and escape the stress once in a while so that you can be more prepared to weather the storms that will come again.

An Anchoring
PRAYER

Dear Lord,

I'm so very grateful for the gift of my children. Thank you so much for giving them to me; for their unique personalities; for all they add to my life. Father, help me remember the way you love me as I'm parenting them. Please help me draw from you and remember your Word, to be gentle and kind toward them. Lord, let me extend to them all the love you offer me—let that love pour through me, so it's not something I have to work to drag up out of my own emptiness, but rather an experience of your overflowing. You are the kindest Father. Help me be a kind mother. In Jesus' name, Amen.

An Anchoring
SCRIPTURE

So, as those who have been chosen of God, holy and beloved, put on a heart of compassion, kindness, humility, gentleness, and patience. . . . In addition to all these things put on love, which is the perfect bond of unity.

COLOSSIANS 3:12, 14

When we think of compassion, kindness, humility, gentleness, patience, love, and unity, we may find ourselves inwardly flailing a bit as these are qualities so seldom seen in the world around us. Read through this Scripture again slowly, pausing occasionally, asking God to let it sink into your soul. Notice that first we are reminded that we are able to behave this way because we are ones who have been chosen by God, holy and beloved!

Which of the qualities mentioned in this verse are most difficult for you to express? Are any of them perhaps particularly important to apply when dealing with one or more of your children?

An Anchoring
ACT

Go back and write down this Scripture (it will help it sink into your heart!) and set aside a time to read it to your family. Talk about what each of these words means, and ask what it would look like if everyone in your house were to live this way. Choose one word to practice this month. Pray together that God would help you do so. Write down your family's observations.

NINE

IRPs Will Happen

Storms created by critical and difficult people

For to this you have been called, because Christ also suffered for you, leaving you an example, so that you might follow in his steps. He committed no sin, neither was deceit found in his mouth. When he was reviled, he did not revile in return; when he suffered, he did not threaten, but continued entrusting himself to him who judges justly. He himself bore our sins in his body on the tree, that we might die to sin and live to righteousness. By his wounds you have been healed.

1 Peter 2:21–24 ESV

Skillful pilots gain their reputation from storms and tempest.

Epicurus

Many years ago, just when I needed a support system, the mother of one of my best friends played a sort of grandmother role to my children once in a while. She lived two hours from our home, but she invited me to come for a weekend so she could "spoil" my children. Southern fried chicken and "Larla's brownies" were always on the weekend menu.

What a grace it was to me during a lonely, discouraging season of my life. My father was dying, Clay and I were only making $600 a month, and we were praying fervently about decisions we needed to make for our future that were scary and entailed a lot of risk. The stakes were high, I was mothering three young children, and there were just so many difficult details in our lives at the time.

I called Clay as I was getting ready to come home from the trip to tell him how much fun we had, and how refreshing the time had been for all of us. Clay didn't seem to hear me, as he responded, "Sally, did you have some kind of argument with XXXXX before you left? She called me and said she hated you and did not ever want to talk to you again, and she is going to be talking to leadership about why they should not allow you to teach the Bible study anymore."

Stunned doesn't even begin to define the depths of my surprise. This was a friend with whom I regularly met for coffee. I had just thrown a party to celebrate her birthday. I could not have been more surprised. I even asked Clay if he was confused and was mistaking her for someone else.

A catastrophic season followed. I was heartbroken, deeply hurt to my core. Her gossip, hatred, and jealousy of the response to my growing Bible study caused her to spread rumors and dissension to others. It was a horrible, terrible, nightmare-style time in my life.

Blows from Other Christians Hurt the Most

One of my biggest challenges in this very fraught and emotional storm was that as a youngish, naïve believer, I didn't know some of the worst hurts in my life would come from other women who called themselves Christians. If someone knew and loved God, wouldn't they be constrained to move in the direction of love, peacemaking, and unity?

I hate to say it, but this storm was only one of several similar ones we experienced in our years of ministry. Before this situation, I had never heard of borderline personality disorder, narcissistic personality disorder, nor many other emotional disorders that drive people to personal destruction. I had never met someone who could lie without having any pangs in their conscience concerning the way others would be affected by their untruths. If I had understood the nature of others more, or pondered the many passages and stories in the Bible that warn of the injustices that happened to others, perhaps I would have weathered it better. After all, it was the most religious people who initiated the condemnation and crucifixion of Christ—the Pharisees, who considered themselves the most righteous of all.

Some of the worst hurts in my life would come from other women who called themselves Christians.

After this out-of-the-blue, irrational attack happened to us in various guises several times over our forty-six years in ministry, we gave those who instigated them a name. We designated them "IRPs"—I-Rational People (with an S at the end, since it was obviously plural!) Amongst our family, we called these interesting experiences "the IRPs and downs of life." We would even say to one another, "I have been IRP-ed again!"

One of my sweet friends was blasted recently by a "well-meaning" friend about her lovely daughter, whom the woman told her was "too quiet" and "socially unacceptable." This child, by God's design, is simply a thoughtful introvert and reader, a creative type. The criticism was unjust, totally opinion-based rather than factual, and hurtful to both mother and child. I have received all sorts of comments about my own imperfect children along the way, as well as attacks on myself from many people I have never even met. What makes people think it is acceptable to openly criticize and judge others, whether in person, in a gossip situation, or online, when Jesus has called us to love, to speak graciously, to encourage one another, and on and on? "Do not judge, so that you will not be judged" from Matthew 7:1 was one of the first verses I memorized as a child. Have we forgotten this command? I have seen that I, too, have a tendency to judge and misunderstand others.

Criticism hurts all of us, and there are all sorts of people out there who want to make us feel inadequate about ourselves, our marriages or lack thereof, our mothering, our housework, our finances—the list goes on and on. Unfortunately, this includes people in church circles who are out to harm us and tear down our reputations.

Often, we are reticent to speak of the hurts we hide inside. We know God hates gossip, and we want to avoid spreading rumors. But I think we also tend to stuff these hurts because if we are in ministry or leadership for very long, we may come to distrust people, never knowing where a critic is going to come from. We also secretly fear that others might think we somehow deserve the painful situation we are dealing with, or that the critic might be just in what they've said. We don't want to risk someone else thinking less of us in a world where close friendship is hard to find. We also second-guess ourselves and ponder, "Am I guilty? Did I do something to deserve this?"

Churches have split, ministries have been divided, marriages have been broken, and children have given up their faith because of the hatefulness of critical, fault-finding believers. Divisiveness is hateful to God, yet it happens all the time.

I wanted to address this area of difficulty because many of us have been deeply disheartened and almost stopped in our tracks by gossiping, lying, or critical people. Sometimes, these are family. I, too, have experienced this in family. I understand, and I am so sorry. But you must know there is a way to recover and restore from such emotional abuse. I am not trying to give reductive, easy answers. I do think we sometimes bear scars and disabilities through our lives that have been created by the havoc of such spiritual, emotional, and physical abuse.

Divisiveness is hateful to God, yet it happens all the time.

Growing through the Storms

I have found there is a way by God's grace to leave the vestiges of a storm's rage behind and to rebuild. I wish these terrible storms had never happened and we had never had to live through them, and especially not multiple times in totally different places. But I also know now that difficult relationships are a tempest in life that many mature people have withstood, coming out stronger and more prepared to keep going.

Sadly, others have become victims of people's jealousy, criticism, and hatred. We must determine to be among those who come through the storms stronger rather than succumb to the fury.

As we think about overcoming in this area, let us consider Jesus (always a good idea!). We read in 1 Peter 2:21–23: "Christ also suffered for you, leaving you an example, so that you might follow in his steps. He committed no sin, neither was deceit found in his mouth. When he was reviled, he did not revile in return; when he suffered, he did not threaten, but continued entrusting himself to him who judges justly" (ESV).

Jesus was perfect. He never sinned or made a mistake, and yet He was unjustly accused, sentenced, and condemned to the worst kind of death. And Peter tells us He is our example to follow. This verse comes to me all the time, especially this phrase: "When he was reviled, he did not revile in return; . . . but continued entrusting himself to him who judges justly."

What does His attitude say? We do not have to carry the poison of a person who has unjustly hurt us. We can give it to God. We can tuck it into the file drawer of heaven and let Him ultimately deal with it. There have been times when I carried around something someone said, rehearsed it over and over again, shook my fist at the injustice

We do not have to carry the poison of a person who has unjustly hurt us.

of it all, and the result? It poisoned me and ate me up emotionally. But Jesus gives another way—give it up and leave it to God. He will justify you in time.

Consider His Servant, Job

Perhaps being misunderstood and misjudged is one of the major storms we will go through. There was another whose story we read in the Old Testament who was unjustly criticized—and he was one the best of humans who walked the earth (Job 1:6–12).

For many years now, I have contemplated Job's story. Job was a man chosen by God as a model of righteousness. We read in the book bearing his name that God trusted Job to be faithful in the midst of Satan throwing the worst into his life. After Job's children, servants, and livestock were all killed, Job's friends suggested he must have secretly been evil and that is why his life was being destroyed. The reality was that everything happening had been instigated by the enemy to tempt Job to turn against God. He isn't the only one, either—we see in Scripture that Jesus was tempted before His ministry began and Peter was tempted before he became the leader of the disciples, and so will we all be. It is a common biblical theme.

In the midst of his trials and suffering, Job's friends pontificated—elaborated in confident tones and words—about why Job was suffering. Most of their opinions were utter foolishness. They judged Job's life and criticized him. Their words had the effect of discouraging Job and making him introspective, even though he was in this spiritual battle after being pointed out for his righteousness.

What do these stories teach me to help me prepare to better sail through storms? That the righteous—and yes, that means you, if you are seeking to walk with God—will be judged wrongly and tempted by Satan in many ways.

If we desire to live righteously by faith in this present day, we will have to make decisions that go against the norm of most people. Consequently, we are always going to have "Job's friends" in life. IRPs seem to be everywhere!

The righteous will be judged wrongly and tempted by Satan in many ways.

No matter how diligent you are or how much work you do, you and your spouse and children are going to behave in an embarrassing manner or an immature way or blunder at some point in your life. You will violate someone else's standard, probably more than once! And your "Job's friends" will be sure to notice and to tell you what you are doing wrong or how unsocialized your child is or how their children are much more advanced than yours, or whatever.

Handling Unjust Criticism

In my journal, I have written some lessons I have learned over the years to help me move beyond bitterness and into the peace of God as it applies to unjust critics:

1. God is your audience, and He is on your side. I am so thankful that I finally came to understand and believe my true audience was God. He knows me and my limitations and the limitations of my family

and children, and He is still on my side. He strongly supports those whose hearts are completely His. Also, He is mindful that we are but dust! His love is unconditional—not dependent on our becoming perfect before He bestows it. He just loves us because His very nature is love.

2. We are not responsible for other people's irrationality or bad attitudes. They were already immature, or critical, or just plain mean before they ever got to us. If we have people in our lives who behave this way, discouraging us on a regular basis, we must understand we need to deflect their "bites" because they are flawed, and taking them on or trying to change them is not our responsibility but God's. To be able to throw off the pain caused on a regular basis by some people frees me from engaging every time they throw out a bid for conflict. I just don't accept the bid.

3. I hate to even say this, but critics are sometimes just a fact of life. If I accept this as a part of life, I am not drawn as personally into the conflict. The storms that rise are not as devastating if I have learned to expect them. Seasoned sailors are those who have passed through many storms and understand the nature of them. And of course, what parent has not heard the criticism from a child? A hormonal teen? A frustrated adult child?

4. It also helps me to remember that since I don't have perfect awareness of anyone's story, there may very well be layers of buried hurt causing the bitterness and anger some people express. Asking God to let me

see them through His eyes, remembering that pain causes people to lash out, and trying to act in love as I respond goes a long way. My goal of loving people in their authentic context has increased as I have gotten older. Perhaps I am more grateful that, in spite of my flaws, God has forgiven me and always accepts me, warts and all. And so I know that others would like to have that from me.

I have learned that before I get up to speak, someone in the audience is already against me or doesn't like my choice of dress or something. One year at a MomHeart conference, a woman said to me, "When you wore that red dress last year, I just knew the messages would not be quite as deep; since you have on a blue dress this year, I think they will be wonderful!" (What does that even mean?!)

I have often told my children that when you stand up for something, you become a bigger target. When you seek to lead, even if it's merely by living a different sort of life from the norm, you offer more for people to shoot at. It is just part of putting our ideals out there.

From time to time, I am sorely tempted to quit ministry. If I listened to every critical comment that was made to me, I would have given up my ministry and my ideals long ago. (To be fair, I receive so many thoughtful, encouraging comments—of which I am unworthy—that inspire and encourage me to go on!)

If I listened to every critical comment that was made to me, I would have given up my ministry and my ideals long ago.

However, I have learned that I am free in Christ to like who

He has made me, to love and believe in my children as they are (even with all their obvious flaws), and to be patient and grateful with the husband I have been given—because He who began a good work in all of us has promised to complete it in Christ, eventually, little by little (Philippians 1:6).

"I know whom I have believed and am persuaded that He is able to keep what I have committed to Him until that Day" (2 Timothy 1:12 NKJV). If I had given in to all the insecurities and inadequacies I have felt before others, I would have given up on this road a long time ago and failed in actually obeying Christ.

What About Mental Illness and Irregular People?

Scripture tells us: "Behold, I am sending you out as sheep in the midst of wolves; so be as wary as serpents, and as innocent as doves" (Matthew 10:16).

Sometimes I forget this verse. Jesus is sending us as sheep to a host of wolves. Wolves love to devour sheep. They are clever enemies and find many ways to trap their game. I think Jesus wanted His disciples to know they would encounter people whose motives were not pure; people who could potentially eat them up (metaphorically, of course).

If I am to weather storms of life that include or are caused by supposed believers, wolves wrapped in sheep's clothing (Matthew 7:15), I must be on the alert. "Be wise as serpents [snakes]" (Matthew 10:16, ESV), as Jesus said. Be intuitively looking for the fruit people produce. If their lives produce division, discouragement, gossip, and lies, then Jesus has already warned you to avoid them.

A seasoned sailor is one who knows how to evaluate a storm and what to do. I was so naïve when I was a young believer, I didn't know to be on guard. I was not educated about all the possibly abusive avenues a relationship could take, or the many mental disorders people may have that predispose them to lying, manipulating, exaggerating, accusing, and all sorts of negative, harmful practices in relationships. As a family, we have been caught in the throes of several such relationships where we just assumed that since we as believers did not feel it was acceptable to lie, others would not, either.

Now, through experience, we know to be cautious with new people in our lives, especially when trusting them with big areas of responsibility or in regard to our intimate relationships.

There is another admonition in Matthew 10:16: "Be innocent as doves." In other words, Jesus does not want us to retaliate, but He wants us to be innocent in our behavior. Not an eye for an eye, but instead offering forgiveness, mercy, and humility as an ultimate response.

Boundaries have to be set in our lives. We do not have to acquiesce to every request people make. We are free, by faith, to evaluate whether a relationship is harmful for us and to pull back or avoid such a relationship. We must learn to take people in their context, to find out their story and background, to understand why they behave as they do. It is an act of faith to proceed in the world of difficult relationships. We are called to love one another. We are told to forgive. Yet we are also called to be discerning. And we must remember that gossip is abhorrent to God. And, neither I nor you is called to save the whole world and everyone we meet. Only Christ can do that.

I have been the brunt of gossipers on numerous occasions. Usually, they are people who have not even talked with me and often they are jealous or critical of my ministry. It has hurt me and my children many times. Proverbs tells us in many verses that God hates gossip. It is utterly wrong to spread hatred or a false opinion about a person with others. And the excuse "I was just sharing" is not acceptable to God. Anything that separates one from another—that perpetuates thinking less of someone—is sinful and creates havoc, and it is not acceptable to our Lord. We need to be able to unload our hearts to those who are trustworthy and in our inner circles. But slander, spreading words of harm, judging others is not allowed in Scripture.

So, as a life commitment, we must love people as much as possible and understand that no one we ever meet will be perfect, and often we are subject to immaturity because of brokenness in our backgrounds. There are people who would be dangerous for me to walk in covenant with—wolves in sheep's clothing. Yet, I have decided to obey what God desires: "If possible, so far as it depends on you, be at peace with all people" (Romans 12:18).

"If it is possible"—in other words, Paul leaves the window open to help us understand that *it may not always be possible.* When I have had big, dramatic separations from individuals where relationships were not healthy, I have learned over time to leave it in God's hands. To seek to make peace as I can. To humble myself if I had any part in the rift. And to determine to forgive and be kind and civil if our paths ever cross again. I really don't want Satan to use these relationship storms to discourage me from writing or speaking that might help others. We must determine to keep going forward.

When a rift is inevitable, praying for the person and seeking not to hold on to it is important. Of course, I am summarizing as though it is simple. In some ways it is simple, but that doesn't make it easy. It's hard to be humble, to forgive, and to leave it to God to justify us. Yet when we carry bitterness, accusation, and/or a desire to retaliate, it just poisons and drains us. Remember, as we read earlier, "When he was reviled, [Jesus] did not revile in return; . . . but continued entrusting himself to him who judges justly" (1 Peter 2:23 ESV).

Because I understand the brokenness of people more, I seek to lay a foundation of healthy relationships with healthy people as my inner circle, so that I will have support and accountability. Then I freely reach out with the love of Christ wherever I can, while using discernment as I seek to minister to those who need the love, compassion, and redemption of Christ. We must seek to cultivate compassion for people in their brokenness if we are ever to show the redeeming love of Christ to a dark and broken world.

> *We must seek to cultivate compassion for people in their brokenness if we are ever to show the redeeming love of Christ to a dark and broken world.*

What about my own people? All of us are in process. All of us are immature at times. Looking for ways to connect, to make peace, to cover a "multitude of sins" (1 Peter 4:8) is a principle I try to live by. What everyone—your husband, teenagers, toddlers—needs is someone who can look deep into their hearts and see beyond their thorns, and say, "Oh, you're expressing a need to me. You're a unique person. This is what motivates you differently than everyone else in our family. If I just wait long enough, tell you I love you, and give you compassion, that will go a lot further than if I spend my time arguing with you."

This whole area of loving people, discerning IRPS, forgiving, setting boundaries, and understanding doves and wolves, is quite complex. Yet, I know with each year, with each experience, I am living more into the mercy and compassion of God and learning how to extend His grace, even to those who have hurt me, because it is for my own well-being and for theirs. May God grant you supernatural wisdom to know how to ford these streams and to find His peace in the midst of each relationship.

An Anchoring
PRAYER

Heavenly Father, how we need you to fill our souls with grace for all the difficult people who fill our lives sometimes with confusion, sometimes with chaos, sometimes with pain. You know what it is to be misunderstood and betrayed, and you know what is in the hearts of all men. Lord, help us. Take our hurt feelings and our frustration, our weakness and tendency to want to give up when we shouldn't—or to hang on when we shouldn't. Let our interactions with others always glorify you. Help us reject remarks made by those who only mean to hurt us, and help us not return evil for evil. We are so glad you know us so well, Lord, and accept us as we are. Thank you for bearing our pain and being our truest Friend. In the name of the One who came to walk among us, Amen.

An Anchoring SCRIPTURE

But I say to you who hear, love your enemies, do good to those who hate you, bless those who curse you, pray for those who are abusive to you. Whoever hits you on the cheek, offer him the other also; and whoever takes away your cloak, do not withhold your tunic from him either. Give to everyone who asks of you, and whoever takes away what is yours, do not demand it back. Treat people the same way you want them to treat you. If you love those who love you, what credit is that to you? For even sinners love those who love them. And if you do good to those who do good to you, what credit is that to you? For even sinners do the same. And if you lend to those from whom you expect to receive, what credit is that to you? Even sinners lend to sinners in order to receive back the same amount. But love your enemies and do good, and lend, expecting nothing in return; and your reward will be great, and you will be sons of the Most High; for He Himself is kind to ungrateful and evil people.

LUKE 6:27–35

This passage, part of the famous Sermon on the Mount, to me seems one of the most convicting and difficult-to-follow parts of Scripture! It is very clear here that Jesus expects me to be-have toward other people in a way that is not natural to me, and that will require a lot of effort if I am to obey His words. I have to remind myself that we are called to behave this way—we are enabled to behave this way—because this is the nature of God toward us, and He will live this way through us as we allow His Spirit to reign in our thoughts and actions. He loved us when we were His enemies; He is good even to those who hate Him; He blesses us and provides for us and gives us everything; He even offers himself.

Who do you find to be the most challenging person in your life? Thank God for them today.

Think about someone who has hurt you and ask Him to help you forgive by writing a short prayer in the lines below.

An Anchoring
ACT

Choose someone you would list in one of the above categories—
irrational, dealing with illness, hurting—and pray for them. Forgive
them. Trust in God that He will bring about good as you intentionally act in obedience. Know that when you do not revile in
return, but trust God (1 Peter 2:23) you are learning to walk the
same pathways that Jesus walked.

TEN

Be Gentle with Yourself

You are worthy of care

You have also given me the shield of Your salvation,
And Your right hand upholds me;
And Your gentleness makes me great.

Psalm 18:35

No way out but through the storm now.

Lisa Wingate

The seventh month of Covid found me living in my small home in Oxford, locked down with my husband, Clay. Stores and restaurants were closed, and we were not allowed to meet with others or congregate in any way—no church, parties, meetings, Bible studies, or social gatherings. Worst of all, no café where I could meet a friend and chat about life. This was not what we had expected. When we closed up our Colorado house and rented one in Oxford—moving over for a season with only a small amount of our earthly goods because the space was so much more limited—we hoped to have gatherings in our home, meeting with people to train them and become part of conferences and retreats. This is what we had planned when envisioning this mini-move almost a year before.

Yet, there we were. Alone, again. Thanksgiving with all of our kids in the UK was canceled. There was no possibility for personal ministry, just trying to figure it all out and understand what the restrictions would mean for us in the months to come. What about the Christmas we had planned for all of our kids in Oxford? Would it be canceled, too?

My life was in some ways so very quiet in lockdown, but still I was trying to make Clay feel happy amidst all of the sequestering, and his ever-present self added hours of companioning him that neither of us was used to since we were both stuck inside—together, every day, all the time! I spent days on end reaching out to my children, who seemed to want to talk hours and hours each week, often daily, since they were alone, too. But we could go nowhere. And in the midst of it, I was in need of making some long-term and short-term decisions for our family.

As I cuddled and wiggled into my soft, warm, squishy duvet a bit more one early morning, pondering all these things, with this book deadline looming, I took a look at my heart-feelings. They were very slow and tired and a little fretful. I lay there feeling I needed to make progress on at least some of these big decisions, because a number of people were waiting on me. My mind was overwhelmed by still-unanswered questions about the future, my children's health, tumbled-around finances, and how all of this would be affected by lockdown, not to mention the state of our crazy world and country . . . there was so much I couldn't do anything about! Suddenly, as though a whisper, the message came: *Be gentle with yourself today.*

Suddenly, as though a whisper, the message came: Be gentle with yourself today.

God seemed to be whispering to me, "Don't make this day the one where you get everything done, figure life out, take care of everyone else in the world. Just be still, just rest, just breathe in peace." This was the message that filled my heart.

So I eased into my morning with gentle, soft music playing; my favorite china mug filled with hot, steaming tea; a candle in a crystal jar; and a view to my living, green garden. *Ahhh, peace.*

For many years I lived as a Martha, rushing around, busying myself, planning more than I could possibly accomplish and then getting grumpy with the kids when life didn't go as planned. I could see how fruitless and wasted this attitude was. Something pushed me, perhaps guilt, to work harder, push more, and get more done.

Little by little, over years, I learned that I cannot ever control life. I am not in charge of the universe, and children and computers and people do not just easily and naturally conform to Sally's expectations and demands! I wasted so much energy and emotion over all the years being a bit anxious and demanding when life did not go as I expected—and it almost never did.

I know now that life will blast my expectations, children will get ear infections at the wrong time, a professional opportunity will not work out, a publisher will fall through on promises, a child or husband will sometimes lash out, friendships will come and go. I don't always get my way, even from a God who loves me, and storms are going to come again. Sometimes, the best thing we can do at times like this is to sleep or rest.

God Was Gentle with Elijah

Many years ago, Elijah became a character I would ponder to help me grow in the direction of valuing slowing down, gentleness, and rest.

Elijah, one of the greatest prophets and leaders in all of Israel's history, had been faithful to God and cultivated faith and faithful acts for decades. In 1 Kings 18, Elijah accomplished the biggest feat of his life—he disproved the existence and power of Jezebel's god. He called down God's power from heaven, defeated all of her prophets, and amazed all of the people in his kingdom.

Yet we read at the end of the story that Jezebel threatened his demise, to take his life:

Ahab told Jezebel everything that Elijah had done, and how he had killed all the prophets with the sword. Then Jezebel sent a messenger to Elijah, saying, "So may the gods do to me and more so, if by about this time tomorrow I do not make your life like the life of one of them." And he was afraid, and got up and ran for his life and came to Beersheba, which belongs to Judah; and he left his servant there. But he himself went a day's journey into the wilderness, and came and sat down under a broom tree; and he asked for himself to die, and said, "Enough! Now, LORD, take my life, for I am no better than my fathers."

1 Kings 19:1–4

Elijah was afraid . . . and ran for his life? After all the miracles he had seen? After the defeat of the prophets of Baal? What's happening here? Suddenly, after all these victories, Elijah crumbled. We read:

Then he lay down and fell asleep under a broom tree; but behold, there was an angel touching him, and he said to him, "Arise, eat!" And he looked, and behold, there was at his head a round loaf of bread baked on hot coals, and a pitcher of water. So he ate and drank, and lay down again. But the angel of the LORD came back a second time and touched him, and said, "Arise, eat; because the journey is too long for you." So he arose and ate and drank, and he journeyed in the strength of that food for forty days and forty nights to Horeb, the mountain of God.

1 Kings 19:5–8

Elijah is one of the most faithful and one of the most valiant heroes of faith in the Old Testament. He was faithful in a pagan land. Faithful when lonely. Faithful in a battle against godless leaders screaming at him of his worthlessness. He was faithful in spiritual battle. And then, as a mere human being at his limits, adrenaline on the ground, he suddenly felt overwhelmed with the desire to give up. He had had enough.

Sometimes it is not the big, cataclysmic event that destroys us, it is the proverbial straw that breaks our back. We just suddenly come to our limit, the last straw. Have you felt like that?

I've had enough of this marriage,
This child,
This church,
This friendship,
These friends,
This job,
This ministry,
This . . . fill in the blank.

Even the most spiritual people become exhausted and depleted and feel like the only way forward is to give up—to give up an ideal, a relationship, a ministry, a commitment. All of us have been dragged around the block a few times over the course of our lives, and we are understandably drained and a little weary.

When we feel this way, what we need is touch, sleep, and rest.

The Power of Touch

I noticed after Elijah poured out his doubts and discouragement to God, God did not say, "Elijah, you need to trust me more. You need to get up and do more. You are disappointing me."

Instead, we read, an angel touched him.

The power of touch and affection is real and created by God to be a comfort to us, physically and emotionally. I remember one time when because of really draining and difficult circumstances, I felt hopelessly depressed. A friend shared my grief and struggle and said, "I don't know what to do to help you. But I can at least provide you with a coupon to get a massage."

I dragged myself to the massage clinic. The lights were lowered, soft music played, and for an hour, every sore muscle, every tender place that was tight, was massaged and felt the deep comfort of a skilled person who knew exactly how to relieve the tension stored up in my body. Oddly, when I got home, I thought, "Hmmm, I don't feel as depressed now." *Nothing had changed*, but somehow just a little deep touch and peaceful quiet had deeply ministered to me so I could go on one more day.

> *The power of touch and affection is real and created by God to be a comfort to us.*

Next the Angel Said, "Arise, Eat!"

Eating can be such a gift—to satisfy our longings in a creative way, to enjoy something tasty or delightful to look at can help pull us out of our glum puddle. Because we are physical beings, we expend energy and strength every waking moment. God made food for our pleasure and He gave us an appetite. He made it necessary for us to eat in order to stay alive. As the primary cook in my home, I am used to having to figure out what everyone wants to eat, every day, all the time. All those meals must be shopped for, cooked, and then, of course, cleaned up after.

During one of my own Elijah seasons, imagine my deep gratefulness when I rolled over one early morning and heard some noise at my door. There, the most beautiful tray was miraculously heading toward my bed. A single dark red rose (my favorite) was tucked into a tiny crystal vase, and a soft flame swayed about, giving out vanilla scent from a small votive candle. Scrambled eggs bedecked with cheese, freshly cooked bacon, and a dollop of sour cream with avocado slices adorned the plate. A separate plate held a pile of raspberries, salted almonds, and a buttered piece of toast literally dripping with goodness. Hot tea steamed from my favorite cup. Sarah and Joy were walking side by side, seeking to keep the tray from tipping over.

"Mama, you serve us every day. We hoped this would cheer you up and let you know we appreciate you."

The food tasted better because someone else had prepared it just for me. And surprise, surprise—they learned how to be tray makers from me! There had been many a surprise tray for them over the years, and they began to make them themselves.

I have to admit, however, that in the vast majority of hard seasons, no one was there to massage my back or to cook for me. The example of an angel serving Elijah has spoken personal permission to my conscience, and I have been known to take myself out to a lovely French brunch or an extravagant meal eaten all by myself in times I knew I just needed some spoiling. I served myself! (Then, of course, there have been seasons when I had to pay for braces or the repair on the washer, and my little joys were more inexpensive but still necessary.)

Should I feel guilty for spending money on myself when there are so many in need? There have been times in our family when we did not know whether the next paycheck would be enough, as our ministry seemed to run out of money every August. But because we have not had lots of family around us most of our lives—and often no close friends, having moved so often—I considered that in their absence and the absence of their care, maybe one of the wisest things I could do was to spoil myself on occasion in order to keep going.

So I had a little box hidden in my desk. Throughout the year, whenever I had an extra bit of cash or someone sent me a check for Christmas or a birthday, I put the money in that box and never allowed it to be put into the grocery fund. It was an emergency reserve just for me, to spend as I pleased. I used the money in this special box once in a while to take a break, to do something fun, or to spoil one of my friends or children. And I don't feel guilty. This little box is like discovering a hidden treasure and has given me moments of reprieve over the years just when I needed it. I suppose you might say I have learned the secret of dancing through life by creating beauty, celebrating small moments, and grasping for joy every day. It is a life commitment and decision to move forward in this way.

> *One of the wisest things I could do was to spoil myself on occasion in order to keep going.*

He Lay Down under the Broom Tree and Fell Asleep

Ahhh, sleep. Don't ever underestimate the power of sleep. I am not a great sleeper. I get very tired, but I am an early riser due to the demands of my parenting-professional life and make a habit of making myself get out of bed to "get to work." Sometimes I have felt that if I am not working in some way, I should feel guilty.

Yet, the past few years, I have made time to sleep in at least one or two days a week. (Clay used to encourage me to do this when the kids were littles, just to help me stay alive.) I remind myself that sleep and rest are actually gifts to those around me because I will be happier, healthier, and stronger longer. Research also tells us that sleep is an important foundation for long-term health and resistance to disease. Sleeping must be a priority when possible.

Other Ways to Be Gentle with Yourself

So, we know that we need to focus on touch, eating, and sleeping in order to be gentle with ourselves. A few other ways to treat yourself in gentleness are:

- Accept your limitations with no shame. No one is perfect. God understands and knows this, and if you choose to understand it too, you will be at peace more often in your life.
- Be careful how you talk to yourself. In other words, monitor the voices in your head to be sure they are the loving voice of God, because your self is listening to yourself.
- Let God be gentle with you. Picture Him as ready to talk, ready to help, ready to give, ready to love you. He is for you. He is not happy about your hurry; He wants you to sit with Him in peace and joy.

His Word Leads the Way

It's important to understand that this admonition to be gentle with ourselves is from God. I have stored up verses to speak to myself in these times. I am reminded, "In repentance and rest you will be saved, in quietness and trust is your strength" (Isaiah 30:15).

As a "good Christian woman," I used to think that if I was truly loving God and walking with Him, I would have a positive, faith-filled attitude all the time. I mean, why not? Generally, I was able to live out this ideal—though sometimes I had to grit my teeth to get there! When difficult situations arose, and my heart began to feel low with my emotions quickly following, guilt for disappointing God would come pointing its finger of accusation, and I would feel disappointed in myself in an existential way.

Now as an older woman, I have become intimately acquainted with the seasons of life. I realize that disappointment in others, disgust with the world's values, and despair arising from some of the raging darkness in the outer as well as inner arenas of my life has been a common experience through the years for myself and others.

A number of other times I felt so discouraged in my life that I felt—for the moment—hopeless and defeated. In one of my favorite books, *Anne of Green Gables*, the kindly older Marilla, who adopted Anne, is talking over a hard situation with her and says, "To despair is to turn your back on God." That statement always made me feel a little guilty, because I felt despair many times in my life. I wondered if I was the only one who felt that way. Yet often when I share these feelings publicly, a woman who hears me will write to me and say, "That is just how I feel! How it helps me to know that others sometimes feel this way, too." It seems there is no escape: if we are alive here on earth, even if we are following God's will to the best of our knowledge and albeit limited ability, difficulty and discouragement and perhaps even depression will be a common part of our lives.

God made me an idealist. I love the idea of life being romantic and everything turning out happily ever after. I would have liked to raise my children in a G-rated world. I would have liked to have a perfect family and good support systems and a really good church fellowship to be a part of, and a warm community who reciprocated to me in friendship and fellowship and no financial stress or relationship stress or health stress or spiritual stress, or basically anything that would cramp my comfort!

Ultimately, this was the hardest thing for me over the years: I just wasn't expecting life to be so hard. I didn't know mothering would be so taxing. I didn't understand that the culture was heading in such a postmodern direction, exactly the opposite direction from that in which Clay and I were leading our family. I also didn't know or understand the constant workload of mothering, and I wasn't trained to do it. One of the most common sources of my difficulty was simply a lack of preparation.

In our world today, we finally seem to understand that depression can be so severe that counseling and medical help need to be sought. We have become more comfortable with the idea of needing that help for our minds and spirits, yet we sometimes ignore the very practical needs of our physical selves. We are triune beings, created in the image of God; we have bodies, souls, and spirits—perhaps more correctly, we *are* bodies, souls, and spirits all in one. This means that as a believer, I must be careful to remember to look at all the issues of my life not only in a material-oriented way but also through a spiritual lens, and see where a lack of spiritual health could be impeding me. I must ask where God might be directing me to pay attention, in the midst of each step of my journey.

> Just as a father has compassion on his children, so the LORD has compassion on those who fear Him.
>
> Psalm 103:13

God understands my depression, regardless of its source. I have realized how important it is for me to know that, contrary to some teachings, He doesn't get some kind of perverted pleasure in watching His sweet children suffer. He is not a detached cosmic being who says, "Okay, now that you have decided to commit yourself to me, I am going to make your life just as hard for you as possible so I can make sure you're serious about it."

He sees us, knows our struggles, weeps with us, and longs to be our comfort. Over the years I have seen that my learning slowly but surely to trust Him more, to lean in more, to understand the nature of the battle one step at a time, has helped me have more strength to fight against the darkness when it comes around once again, as it inevitably will. We all have the capability of moving to stronger places in all areas of our lives, as we

He sees us, knows our struggles, weeps with us, and longs to be our comfort.

persevere and strive to walk all of these difficult paths we face with our eyes on Him, seeking His perspective.

Fixing our eyes on Jesus, the pioneer and perfecter of faith. For the joy set before him he endured the cross, scorning its shame, and sat down at the right hand of the throne of God.

Hebrews 12:2 NIV

It is so helpful to me to read that even Jesus despised the shame of the cross. To get to that point, first He was betrayed by Judas, whom He had been teaching and caring for those three years right alongside His faithful disciples. Then He suffered beating, being spit upon, stripped of His clothing, humiliated. Finally, He endured the excruciating pain of the cross itself. In this Scripture we see that He hated the terrible, humiliating, condescending experience He bore for our sakes—even though He went through it for the sake of what He was able to see before Him.

We see Jesus was a real human, one who wept, became angry, hated humiliation, felt disappointed—and yet, we know He was perfect. We can take comfort knowing that emotional experiences are a part of a healthy reaction to difficult things we experience in life. Finding our hope, again, in Him is part of the journey that leads us gently and slowly out of despair.

The grace of God's Spirit reminds me by so many stories through Scripture that He understands the fatigue that accompanies daily life in a fallen world. He has compassion as a response to my needs. And here is my hope: He prays for me, He supports me by His love and care, and He is gentle with me. Therefore, I need to be gentle with myself.

And now, I think I shall go eat three dark chocolate salted almonds—I am quite sure they are good for me. How about you?

An Anchoring
PRAYER

Dear Heavenly Father,
I am so grateful that you know my weariness. You know all the reasons I feel exhausted and depleted, defeated and too tired to go on. I thank you for the example of Elijah, and the way you sent an angel to minister to him through touch, food, and rest. Please show me how I might offer myself these same graces today, knowing they come from you! Show me how to care for myself, and remind me to even try to put some of these helps into my life before I reach the breaking point next time. In the precious name of Jesus I pray. Amen.

An Anchoring
SCRIPTURE

For even when we came into Macedonia our flesh had no rest, but we were afflicted on every side: conflicts on the outside, fears inside. But God, who comforts the discouraged, comforted us by the arrival of Titus; and not only by his arrival, but also by the comfort with which he was comforted among you, as he reported to us your longing, your mourning, your zeal for me; so that I rejoiced even more.

2 CORINTHIANS 7:5–7

Does it surprise you to read that Paul felt depressed and needed comfort?

Is this a season of darkness and difficulty in your life, or are things going well? If they are going well, do you sometimes still find yourself feeling exhausted? When you find yourself in the midst of conflict or fearful, do you feel guilty about those feelings?

If the answer to either of the above is yes . . . why?

An Anchoring
ACT

Spend some time pondering what fills your cup at this moment in your life—music, a meal out, time alone, hiking, time with a friend? Make a plan in your calendar to include these small breaks regularly. Then, think about someone in your life who is facing a difficult time. Write their name and their needs in the space below. Take a few minutes to pray for them, and then send them a physical note to let them know you did so. Add anything else God puts on your heart that might be comforting to them, as Titus comforted Paul. Also write down one thing you could do to care for yourself this week.

ELEVEN

Weathering a Lifetime of Storms Brings Character and Wisdom

For I am convinced that neither death, nor life, nor angels, nor principalities, nor things present, nor things to come, nor powers, nor height, nor depth, nor any other created thing will be able to separate us from the love of God that is in Christ Jesus our Lord.

Romans 8:38–39

Trying to do the Lord's work in your own strength is the most confusing, exhausting, and tedious of all work. But when you are filled with the Holy Spirit, then the ministry of Jesus just flows out of you.

Corrie ten Boom

A crisp February evening in Oxford found me walking with a bounce in my step to match the mood I carried. On my way to a local store, I searched for a bouquet of flowers that would adequately express my appreciation to my friend for allowing me to stay with her for a couple of weeks before the little old house we were renting was ready for Joy and me to occupy.

Do you ever remember events by the place they were happening? I remember I was rounding a corner on a craggy, uneven sidewalk on my way to dinner with my friend, and my heart was ringing with happiness and confidence. I felt good about having moved to Oxford. I felt it would be a place of friendship, promise, and a budding ministry of outreach to women through my books. I trusted a host of memories to be made in my tiny-but-charming house. I anticipated a year near Sarah's little family and the delight of living with Joy, my kindred spirit and co-adventurer in life. Clay was joining me in just a few days. I was filled with a sense of "This is going to be a place of favor and blessing. I am so grateful to be here."

A lovely dinner and a fun new episode of *Call the Midwife* entertained us, and my friend ventured to make us some coffee. Supposing I could help, I gathered the dishes we had used onto a tray and proceeded to carry them toward the kitchen. Oddly, just at that moment, her huge exercise ball blew into my pathway, pushing against my leg and catching me in a rotating nightmare against her stairs. As I tried to release my leg from the ball by walking forward while still holding on to the tray (*I cannot drop my friend's lovely dishes*, I thought!), the ball rotated with me. After dancing this way for ten feet, I picked up momentum and was propelled across the room.

Finally, I fell forward toward the ground and hit right into the cracked corner of an old table, with my full weight falling on my right eye.

Blood spurted, a small gash below my eye protruded, and immediately I felt excruciating pain as I found myself down on the ground with broken dishes all around me. Literally in the blink of an eye, my eye was injured forever.

I wound up in the emergency room, where I waited four and a half hours before I could be seen and was told I needed an eye specialist. The suggested doctor said my issues were beyond his ability to address. Within a couple of days, I saw a crew of doctors at Moorfield Eye Hospital, a renowned clinic in London. "You have a very serious eye injury; you may lose all of your sight. There is a slice four layers down into your cornea, and it looks like deep infection has grown in the several days since the accident. [It took three days to go through the doctors and tests to determine I needed more specialized help.] We will do our best to save your eye, but we cannot be sure."

The eye eventually became swollen, bright red, and constantly watering, and the situation became a twelve-week event. The doctors prescribed what I now call "poison eye drops," which for the first three weeks I had to use every hour and a half. The drops caused more stinging and raw pain than I ever imagined was possible, as they are similar to bleach being poured onto a wound! I have never before or since experienced such pain. Eventually, I only needed them four times a day. But the swollenness and pain caused by these drops and others I needed caused almost a complete loss of vision for three months. Clay traveled with me by train from Oxford to London twelve weeks in a row to wait long hours in the hospital for treatment. Finally, during the last two weeks, the doctor eliminated the "poison drops" that were like acid on my eye. The doctors ended up saving my eye but reported that my vision would never fully return. Long story short, my vision is permanently impaired, and I already have imperfect vision in my left eye, which must now do most of the work.

Responding to Storms

Oddly, as I look back, I never questioned God or His goodness, or even entertained the idea that He had caused this terrible accident.

We read in Scripture that God cannot be tempted by evil,[1] and I believed God had goodwill for me, as my loving and compassionate Father. I remember at the time, even as I was falling, thinking, *This is spiritual warfare!* It was a clear thought, not a point of panic or fear, just a sort of calm realization.

I am quite visually impaired now. I have trouble when I write or try to look at things far away. Yet, I am just grateful for my one good eye that has provided me with enough vision to write and read. At least I can see.

Over years of such storms, I have learned more and more to relinquish my rights to God and to seek to follow Him through whatever my life brings. A part of growing strong in faith and the character that carries us through the storms is to be able to say to God, "Not my will, but yours be done. Use me for your purposes and your glory. I know that you are the One who is walking with me through this, and you are faithful."

The Lord has stretched me over many years of calamity and storms: car accidents, illnesses of children, church splits, stress, and pressures and conflict of every kind, you name it. But I have learned through all the seasons to expect these storms. I have learned to soldier on, or sailor on, as you will, in this battleground of life. At some point, I planted a flag of faith that said, "From this moment on, I want to survive storms with faith. I want to commit to being an overcomer. I want to please the heart of Jesus, even when I don't understand what is happening." Deciding to stay fast and seeking to be faithful is the way forward for me to live a story worth passing on to future generations.

I have learned more and more to relinquish my rights to God and to seek to follow Him.

We are shaped by our decisions. How important it is that we make commitments and life decisions based on the truth we find in the heart of Christ. We do this by following His example as well as the wisdom in Scripture that the Holy Spirit uses to lead us.

I have learned that life on this earth is in rebellion against God, and I will sometimes be caught in the danger of these violent storms. Yet my place is to face each storm valiantly, with courage sustained by God's Spirit living through me, and with my eyes on Him. I know both from Scripture and from experience that with His grace, I can face each storm with peace in my heart and hope for His loving presence and direction. I know His purposes will be fulfilled through me as I trust these occurrences into His hands and walk with Him.

In plain words, I have learned that storms will come, and Christ asks for my faith as He calms the overwhelming waves and winds that blow my way.

Many people throughout my life abandoned or compromised their faith amidst their own storms, ending up victims of their circumstances. Many gave up their ideals when they became too costly. I did not want to end up cynical, without faith in Christ, or defeated and fearful because of past storms. It is a choice I renew every day: to love and trust God and to live my faith until the day I see Him face-to-face.

Living as a victorious sailor through the storms of life requires the courage to trust Him, the patience to wait it out by His grace, and the strength to find hope and His light in the midst. At the root of this faith is the development and growth of a godly character. Being obedient to God and stretching our character toward holiness does not happen all at once. It grows over time, and is strengthened as we practice using our spiritual muscles to walk with God one day at a time.

One of the by-products of learning how to grow the strength and courage to weather storms well is that our story will encourage others who are struck down in their tracks with unexpected tempests. My children are always, always watching me. We had moved to Oxford to help my daughter Sarah finish her master's in theology. Birthing her first baby meant that Sarah couldn't complete her last year class commitments without help caring for our granddaughter. And so Clay and I made arrangements to come for the time Sarah needed us.

Our story will encourage others who are struck down in their tracks with unexpected tempests.

Months after my accident, Sarah surprised me by writing a blog about what had transpired:

My mom is just about the bravest person I know. Two months ago, after first making a huge move to England to be with me and help me through Lilian's early days, having just seen me through Lilian's adventurous, snow-bestormed birth and the stressful early days of nursing, my mom catastrophically injured her eye. She randomly tripped one evening and fell straight on her eye, landing with her full weight on the sharp corner of a table. The injury was severe; a deep cut, a corneal ulcer, and a raging infection within days. Since her injury, my mom has lost most of the sight in her right eye and endured almost constant, throbbing pain, countless early morning trips to a London eye hospital, round-the-clock eyedrops that meant weeks of almost no sleep, and a total inability to read, write, work, or for a while, even watch a movie.

You might think that such an avalanche of trial might get her down. *Not my mom.* I have watched her wrestle through her exhaustion every day, still strolling down to bring me a scone and make me a cup of tea and delight in Lilian's smiles. I've watched her gamely buy sunglasses to wear indoors while determined to keep on cooking us meals and enjoy holding her grandbaby. I've watched her rock back and forth in pain while still managing to keep up a conversation, to laugh, to tell us to light the candles and get the music going. I've watched her struggle toward joy in moments of deep discouragement by remembering Scripture, by opening the windows to the Oxford spring air, by listening to music one more time. Her prognosis is unclear. But not her courage; it's clear and radiant as a diamond. She hopes. She loves. She trusts God to be good.

My mama is a marvel. I wish I could write a more eloquent tribute, but at the moment, I have a baby sleeping in my lap (only place she'd settle today) and I'm typing this with one hand because I dare not move and wake the little (darling) terror. Here's to you, sweet Mama!

I was so very surprised by Sarah's generous article. I will cherish her words for life. But even more, I realized that my story of walking as faithfully as I knew how through the days was having a deep impact on my children. Our children, families, and friends will face many storms. But when we walk through our own with courage and faith, choosing joy, it will become a pattern that they will learn to follow when their lives are confronted by similar difficulties.

A Lesson in Character Growth

Vienna, Austria, is one of my most cherished and beloved places in all the world. Living there for years during my twenties taught me to love tea and coffee times, to engage in history even more, to become international in my heart, and to understand how hungry people are to know the love of God and His purposes for their lives.

One of my favorite places to walk was the *Volksgarten* ("people's garden"). Created and opened for the public in 1821 so everyone would have a lovely place to walk, it has become known for some of the most beautiful gardens in the world.

Once when walking there, I happened upon a wrinkled, leather-skinned-from-so-much-time-outdoors gardener. He proudly spoke to my friend and me about what it cost to cultivate such elegant and flourishing roses. The garden and particularly each plant had to be cultivated over many years to grow so large, always cut back to the nub when growing season was over. It required protection from storms and bugs that would eat away at its roots, and fertilizer and water in the right amount each season. The cultivation of this treasure of plants has not come about by accident, but by careful planning and care over many years, through many differing gardeners who cared that the legacy of gorgeous flowers continued.

The legacy of a godly character, including integrity, righteousness, truth, faithfulness, patience, steadfastness, and humility, is only produced over much time. Seasons of growth take place as we flourish in faith and then move through discipline and spiritual training so we grow even stronger and wiser over time. To mount up over storms with grace requires a godly character produced through gathering experience.

To mount up over storms with grace requires a godly character produced through gathering experience.

Reaping a harvest of character comes from planting seeds of integrity over a lifetime. What you sow you will reap. The amazing result is that you will have fruit for your labor and be satisfied and gratified to see how God has worked with you as you walk in obedience.

Men without Chests

C.S. Lewis is famous for his essay "Men without Chests" from *The Abolition of Man*. In it, he describes a generation of people without virtue or character because of the rise of relativism and loss of objective truth. In the style of the ancients, he describes the head as the place of knowledge, the heart as the place of passion, and the chest as the place of virtue and character.

Only when a person has a well-developed character can they properly put to use knowledge and passion. Without the strength of character developed in the chest, knowledge can become cruel, and passion destructive. With character, knowledge becomes wisdom and passion becomes love.

> Only when a person has a well-developed character can they properly put to use knowledge and passion.

It seems there are many people without chests in our world. With the constant influx of information provided by the internet, and no effective way to clearly determine the objectivity or truthfulness of that information, people can develop keen opinions, but not be required either to validate those opinions or to act on them. In the same way, it is easy for us to voice emotional and idealistic claims without doing the hard work of validating our opinions objectively and putting them into actual practice in our lives.

Opinion has become a substitute for wisdom that only comes from truth, knowledge, experience, and character.

If we are truly to be full-bodied people who act on the biblical ideals that we hold to be objectively true, we must practice integrity based on Scripture and grow the muscle of character. We must become men and women with chests.

Habits Build Character

The essence of character is found in the habitual heart choices of an individual over a long period of time. Character is the constant work of a lifetime and the product of a heart engaged in wisdom, choosing the right thing over and over again. It is like practicing a sport. If you've ever taught a child to catch or throw a ball, you know the moment in which it "clicks." Suddenly, the youngster grows from awkward fumbles to being able to catch the ball almost every time; eventually, snagging the ball out of the air becomes an automatic response. Character is the product of good choices made over and over again, so that when the curveballs of life come your way, you can automatically respond in wisdom because that is what you have practiced.

> *Character is the product of good choices made over and over again.*

What we practice shapes who we become, and the voices we listen to shape what we will practice. If we are to live lives of character, we must invest in wisdom. One of my mentors once gave me a great quote: "God forgives, but wisdom does not." In other words, God is open always to forgiving us of our shortcomings as we confess them to Him, ask for forgiveness, and long for His wisdom. Yet, if I violate wisdom by running a red light, for instance, and cause a wreck and harm to a person, God will forgive me the mistake, but the consequences of a crashed car and damages to another will still be there, and I will be required to pay. The heart of wisdom is properly understanding the impact and meaning of our personal choices. The book of Proverbs very clearly delineates good and bad decisions—a practice that is not popular in our day.

The purpose of Proverbs is not to create strict rules to live by, but to help the reader live a life of wisdom which brings peace. I do not tell my children, "Don't go over the speed limit!" because I like to impose difficult rules upon them, but because if they do go over the speed limit, they will more likely have to pay a ticket or get in a wreck.

Wisdom creates healthy hedges around our behavior, determining what we will and won't do. We obey God's commands in order to build our lives on foundations that will stand and not fail us in the storms of life. We live with virtue so others can look to us as beacons that will show them the love and redemption of God. Our virtue should help in our outreach and draw others to us, not send them away.

Character Builds Integrity

When God called us to be lights in a lost generation, His desire was that, through our virtue, steadfastness, and commitment to purity of life and behavior, we would become guides to those who long to move from darkness into light. Becoming the best you can be requires that you own your integrity, and live the most virtuous life possible.

Because we reflect the character of God, Christians should be the most trustworthy, hardworking, truth-telling, dependable, moral, patient, and grace-filled people. This is our heritage from God.

Our integrity comes before our influence.

Integrity comes from years of practicing living with godly character. It is the lifelong fruit of determining to live faithfully. Christ is the model for what it looks like to have perfect integrity. But integrity brings the reward of living well into your life and watching God faithfully produce eternal fruit through the pages of your story.

Integrity Builds Legacy

Character is the constant work of a lifetime. It is the product of a heart engaged in wisdom and choosing the righteous option of obedience over and over again.

I seem to have plenty of opportunities to practice this principle of character training in my own life right now, as do you. Areas of character that seem particularly useful to me as I look back over the last years of my life are ones I never appreciated when I was younger. Then, I tended to fight against the injustices of life, seeking to control my circumstances. Often, I was deeply discouraged by the injustice of life-storms in a fallen world, especially when other people seemed to get away with murder while I was held accountable to be the "mature" one.

Integrity comes from years of practicing living with godly character.

Pondering these verses one day, I caught a glimpse of life as a more seasoned, storm-trained person.

> Though youths grow weary and tired,
> And vigorous young men [and women] stumble
> badly,
> Yet those who wait for the LORD
> Will gain new strength;

> They will mount up with wings like eagles,
> They will run and not get tired,
> They will walk and not become weary.
>
> Isaiah 40:30–31

There are many potential gifts of aging and gaining experience, yet our culture is not inclined to appreciate the value of age or the richness of wisdom in contrast to the confidence and cleverness of youth. Those who have grown older through many years of ideals and trials, and yet held fast to God, even in the darkness, have bought for their toil perspective, wisdom, humility, and gentleness.

The older one becomes, the more one understands how little power or control we have over life, circumstances, and relationships. The fighting and scrambling for the things of this world, the seeking to make life tame its raging storms, the shaking the fist at heaven becomes futile to one who is focusing on eternity.

Humility grows through a realization of how finite we are and how much we need and depend on God's grace for our very lives. The older I am, the more I am aware of my flawed, self-centered self, and the more grateful I am for God's condescending love, His acceptance of me through all my sin, and His willingness to companion me with His presence.

Gentleness grows because we are ourselves in such need of gentle compassion, mercy, and love from others in our own frailty. We read, "A gentle answer turns away wrath" in Proverbs 15:1 and learn that gentleness calms a broken relationship or even just an irritated moment. Jesus said, "Take My yoke upon you and learn from Me, for I am gentle

and humble in heart, and you will find rest for your souls"
(Matthew 11:29).

Learning to Rest and Wait on God

We need rest on a regular basis. Yet true rest comes from
pondering, understanding, and living into the humble and
gentle heart of Christ—not an angry heart, not a demanding
heart, but one that is gentle and humble.

My daughter Joy and I were walking together in one of
my favorite parks in Oxford. She said, "Mama, I don't think
you doubt the love of God for you because you see Him as
gentle, serving, loving, and *for you.*" I was so touched that
she knew my rest came from dwelling in the center of God's
heart, where His love, mercy, and grace for me are abundant
and never ending. If only more people could understand this
amazing love of God.

Patience and waiting on God are not easy for me. I am
quick, wanting instant results, and I am a Martha-type
person in so much of my life. Yet, because I have learned
that almost nothing happens on my time schedule, and that
I always have to wait for His timing anyway, my spiritual
muscle has been stretched to learn to wait more easily, to
choose to be patient, and to trust that in the end God is
good.

These gifts are only for those who determine to continually chase after Him; those who hold fast, even in the darkness; those who choose to believe when they cannot see.
These gifts from God's hand satisfy and give peace. Working
so hard and performing for others becomes meaningless, and
grace comes in their place.

Those who do not choose to believe in God in the darkness will remain in darkness and despair for life, and build a legacy of disbelief, bitterness, and cynicism. Those who compromise ideals when tempted to conform will have torment and regret. Those who disbelieve in God's goodness and the wisdom of His ways will have bitterness and sourness of soul for a legacy.

Finally, the word *steadfast* has become an important part of how I would describe the character of mature Christians I have observed over time. To be steadfast means to stand fast, unwavering, loyal, trustworthy in all circumstances, through all times. I have recently been pondering how I want this to be something God sees in the commitment of my heart for the rest of my life. I want to be steadfast that others might understand how to remain faithful through their storms.

I want to be steadfast that others might understand how to remain faithful through their storms.

We need others to model this for us that we might know how.

Scripture says, "Blessed is the man who remains steadfast under trial, for when he has stood the test he will receive the crown of life, which God has promised to those who love him" (James 1:12 ESV). If we truly believe in Him and His promises, then every day is a time for us to seek how to be faithful, at peace, strong, and immovable.

Many days when I am in Colorado, if I go outside and drive toward town, the mountains are visible—stable, immovable, and solid. God compares himself to a mountain or rock. I have been pondering this these last days, knowing that as I strain to be more like Him, I, too, can be stable, strong, a refuge for others, dependable, and steadfast.

This is a time to lean into our ability to be strong. We have the capacity, but we must exercise our wills, for the sake of our love for Christ, to wait for Him to direct our lives, not demanding to know and understand everything yet.

Storms are a time for us to act in light of our hope that He is preparing for us a place where all of life will be redeemed. They are a time to show others—our families, children, friends—that our hope is true and sure, not false. We can write the story of our days as ones of growth, strength, love, and beauty because He is "God with us," and He is a rock, immovable, our refuge.

An Anchoring
PRAYER

Dear Heavenly Father,

Thank you so much for your steadfastness, your strength, your stability in my life. Thank you for being so solid and allowing me to depend on you completely. I want my character to be like yours, Lord. Help me to stand on you firmly, in every area of my life; in my marriage, my parenthood, as a friend and co-worker and neighbor. Help me to persevere as I keep my eyes on you, in Jesus' precious name, Amen.

An Anchoring
SCRIPTURE

We who have taken refuge would have strong encouragement to hold firmly to the hope set before us. This hope we have as an anchor of the soul, a hope both sure and reliable and one which enters within the veil.

HEBREWS 6:18–19

What does it mean to you to picture God as steadfast and reliable?

Do you feel this is a quality you already possess?

Looking back over your life, how well are you weathering your storms?

An Anchoring
ACT

A part of character is to be able to say to God, "Not my will, but yours be done. Use me for your purposes and your glory. I know that the One who is walking with me through this is faithful."

Take some time to make a list of various storms you've been through in your life. Beside each, note a lesson you've learned as you made your way through it—even if it was a hard lesson because it seems you didn't manage the storm well at the time. Can you see growth in wisdom over the years? Thank God for the fact that you're still here and seeking Him. Consider writing out a prayer of commitment to continue following Him every day, through every storm, for the rest of your life.

TWELVE

Leaving a Legacy Begins with a Foundation

Do not fear, for I am with you;
Do not be afraid, for I am your God.
I will strengthen you, I will also help you,
I will also uphold you with My righteous right hand.

Isaiah 41:10

There is peace even in the storm.

Vincent van Gogh,
The Letters of Vincent van Gogh

Monday morning, I slipped down the stairs of our little home-away-from-home in Oxford and put on the kettle as usual. The sun was not yet up, so

I lit my dark little room with candles, turned on some soft music, and sat in the gentle quietness of my moment alone to enter the day with grace.

My phone buzzed with a message from my daughter. "Mama, have you seen the news about Shelly? Look in your inbox. I am so sorry. I love you, Mama. Wish I could be with you."

With trepidation, I opened my email and found this note from Shelly's husband:

It is with a heavy heart that I share with you news about Shelly. As most all of you are aware, earlier this year she was diagnosed with a sarcoma tumour. The tumour was removed in May, but the cancer quickly returned aggressively and spreading rapidly.

Late Sunday night, All Saints Day, Shelly died in hospital after developing a vascular bleed related to the cancer. I was able to be with her in her final moments as we talked and prayed together.

I was reminded in those last minutes together of the passage from Psalms 116:15: "Precious in the sight of the Lord is the death of his saints" [ESV]. As we talked, cried, and prayed we rejoiced that she was soon to be in the presence of the Lord.

Shelly never feared death, but she did not want to have to go through a long period of suffering. As we talked last night, we both felt it was God's kindness and grace that she went so quickly and with very little pain. . . .

From the moment I started reading, a sadness began to swell in my heart, deep down. Tears came to my eyes. My sweet friend Shelly was gone. I carried the grief as a weight on my shoulders during the days that followed. The sadness of not being with her again hung with me through the days of my week.

Her death did not take me by surprise, as I had lived through so many deaths of precious ones through so many years. The grief was more like a familiar companion, bringing a heavy burden. I had become personally acquainted with this experience through many sad times. No more was I surprised by deaths, cancers, brain tumors, car wrecks, or suicides. They were never easy, but at some point, I had moved slowly beyond the surprise of death to a quiet acquiescence. Death is the closing of the last chapter in the story of our lives on earth. But we will have more story to live with Him. I have never escaped the deep pain of parting from loved ones, but I have come to understand it. All of our lives as we know them will come to an end.

No more was I surprised by deaths, cancers, brain tumors, car wrecks, or suicides.

In this world, I would miss the ability to take the train to Shelly's London flat, to be greeted with her warm smile, to continue our vibrant companionship over a cup of tea, to know the deep fellowship that grows with one who is truly kindred. Our life values and soul treasures were so akin, and we understood one another without having to explain ourselves. She understood so many ideals of my life that others had not lived, especially when it came to living overseas, living for the kingdom, living to give His love to others. I'll not

quickly forget an evening shared with H, her husband, and
Shelly over the most delicious herbed-baked chicken meal,
candlelight and music setting the tone.

At a time when I felt odd and alone in my perception of
the world, politics, international living, and ministry outreach in the UK, both Shelly and her husband made me feel
deeply companioned in this season of life. Their words spoke
hope and light in deep places where I longed for sympathy
and affirmation.

Yet, even more, Shelly was a friend of delight. From the
first time we met, she brought sunshine with her presence.
She had come to see me in Oxford, and that is when our
friendship began. She had reached out to me, which is not
typically my experience. She had brought beauty, kindness,
and gentleness in a time I needed it. Her friendship was like
a kiss from God.

As the days after her death passed, I found myself coming to a place of thanksgiving, beyond the sorrow. "Thank
you, God, that I had the privilege of knowing Shelly. Thank
you that you gave me a friend who was total grace. Thank you
that her fragrance of joy in life was allowed me, even if for
a short while."

Sometimes you meet someone unexpectedly who is living
the way you hope your life will play out, one who calls you
to your best self. Her legacy of love for God, for her family,
and for her friends was infectious. She made me want to be
better, love God more, be more generous.

Her life reminds me that all of us can become that kind of
person if we choose to travel the path of our lives intentionally, purposefully considering how we want to walk. And
in this process of walking with God through these days, I

remember, once again, how He has gently, lovingly shepherded me through my whole life, through each life storm. God has walked my path with me that I might learn what is of real value; what is true in a fallen world; where my hope is; that His mercy, grace, love, and sympathy are real. Because He cares so much, God has helped me to open my fist and let go of the things I was holding on to so tightly that would never have brought me eternal treasure. He has replaced these idols with true gifts that have served to bring me deep soul satisfaction. He has shaped me through humility that I might depend on Him and not myself, with a longing for His kingdom rule that is surely coming, with a deeper compassion and love for fellow travelers who are yet to understand His abiding deep love and affection. In short, God has become my treasure, my hope, my wisdom. But these treasures were strewn through the pathway of my storms.

All of us can become that kind of person if we choose to travel the path of our lives intentionally, purposefully considering how we want to walk.

How Will I Respond?

Isn't it interesting that though the disciples were taken through the storm on the Sea of Galilee, there were far more dangerous storms to come that would make the first storm seem tame. In the end, all but John (who, it is thought, died naturally, but in exile) would be killed violently for their faith in Christ. They had the honor of giving testimony of His irrefutable existence, His eternal provision for our secure place with Him in eternity. The storm on the lake that night was a training ground for more meaningful storms yet to come. By their endurance through life-storms when Jesus was present with them for three years, they were prepared to endure ultimate violence in their deaths, and each faced those terrible moments with grace and submission, leaving a powerful legacy of faith.

Through years of walking with God through seasons of life-storms, He taught me that I have the prerogative to decide what kind of legacy I will leave, as Shelly did. Her beginnings were harsh, and her story was difficult—even heartbreaking. Her story became a beautiful book narrating her journey from a childhood fraught with pain and disappointment to a life that flourished and brought beauty when she found Christ. *Searching for Certainty* has been a gift to many worldwide. She redeemed her story and made it one of beauty. She decided she would live in the reality of God's light and love and extend it as a life message.

Over the past few years, I have thought a lot about the concept of agency. To have agency means I have the power to determine the choices I make, the way I become a steward of my own story, and the pathway I will take toward the legacy I want to leave. I have the possibility of walking by faith, straining toward a virtuous life, and emulating the power of God's Spirit in and through my life. I also have the agency to deny His goodness, to live defeated, to resist His grace, to rebel against His offer of companionship, or to be a victim of the darkness I see and experience.

No one can make you or me be godly people.

No one can make you or me be godly people. No one can force us to become spiritually responsive. No one can make choices for us to not be bitter or disappointed with others or with our circumstances. *We* must choose, *we* must obey, *we* must move in the direction of wisdom and growing strength.

Most of us want the gold medal; we just don't want to have to endure the training that is required to receive it.

As a young believer, someone told me the story of the Israelites looking toward the fruitful and blessed land that God had decided to provide them as a home, a holding place for His beloved people. God had instructed them through Moses about how to live justly, how to train their children, how to treat one another, how to live in a way that would cause them to flourish. Yet, God said they must *choose*.

The whole passage is worth a long ponder and study. I memorized these verses as a reminder to myself that I had agency to determine the way my life would be lived out.

> See, I have placed before you today life and happiness, and death and adversity, in that I am commanding you today to love the LORD your God, to walk in His ways and to keep His commandments, His statutes, and His judgments, so that you may live and become numerous, and that the LORD your God may bless you in the land where you are entering to take possession of it. But if your heart turns away and you will not obey, but allow yourself to be led astray and you worship other gods and serve them, I declare to you today that you will certainly perish.
>
> Deuteronomy 30:15–18

Always, There Will Be Storms

There will always be storms in our lives. There will always be circumstances, people, and matters of life that threaten to overwhelm us. Perhaps the icy cold fingers of fear squeezing out all the hope in one's heart for what might happen to a child, a job, a marriage, a life; the darkness of depression hanging heavily as a cloud over all the moments of a day; exhaustion and weariness dragging the body stumbling through foggy moments of a difficult season; illness that threatens to overwhelm; a marriage that bruises and wounds deep where no one else sees; bitterness or blame that steals each moment of thought into death and hate; loneliness so palpable and sad; the obscurity of being unknown in life's burdens and ignored and uncared for. All and more of these might be the names of our storms, and yet . . .

The grace and beauty of a woman shows brightly when she decides to stand up to the threats of the giant gales of wind and rain, to stand strong against her would-be foes with tools of heaven's design. This determined one, by bringing order, wisdom, and peace into them, can make the storms of her life into memories of the power of God.

When she understands the importance of civilizing nations by raising strong children of faith in her home, and through strong family relationships, she will indeed find courage to patiently ride out the dark nights of life.

Because of her faithfulness, her legacy will be a future adult generation able to exercise moral courage and fortitude because of the foundation of virtue she carefully laid. Those who remember her strength will exhibit strength of their own in places of leadership because of the example she lived. A valiant woman understands that her children are watching as she chooses to exhibit courage, so that someday, because of her faith and faithfulness, they will know how to be courageous.

And so, we exhibit strength instead of fear, so that some-day those who watch us will be strong. We have to make the choice to believe in God and in His ability to provide for us, because we want those watching to believe in His eventual timely provision.

When we submit to His ways and times, we will be freed to celebrate His goodness in front of our audience who are learning how to live by faith in our presence.

By their observation, those in our lives will understand that though it is natural to whine and complain, or to be selfish and unloving, it is by God's grace that we face storms in all of their fury and wait to see them pass.

> *"You come to me with threats of devastation. But I come to you in the name of the Lord of hosts, and He will protect me, provide for me, and be with me."*

It is not natural, but supernatural, a result of being filled with the Holy Spirit, to praise and be thankful and to choose to express love and faith amid the challenges. It is conviction of His reality that causes us to put one foot in front of the other day after day despite difficulty, and we model faithfulness as a choice.

We look our storms in the face and say, "You come to me with threats of devastation. But I come to you in the name of the Lord of hosts, and He will protect me, provide for me, and be with me—and all His host of angels is on my side."

Choose a Legacy of Hope

This choice to be courageous is beyond our feelings. Even when our emotions don't agree, we can practice as a way of life choosing to live in obedience to what is known about His character, which we believe by faith to be loving and good. These actions are truly supernatural, only possible as we walk in the power of His Holy Spirit. It happens as we say with all our heart, by faith and with the conviction of planting a flag of belief, "He is good. He is faithful and true and He will save me, in His time. I believe all things will work together for good, and I will see it when I am with Him looking at it from His eye-view."

So today, my friend, look for joy. Seek out beauty.

Look at your storms, even in the darkest moments, and claim the victory that is there for the asking. Model to your children what it means to live in celebration of God's marvelous life. Look for the miracles that might otherwise go unnoticed each day.

Look at your storms, even in the darkest moments, and claim the victory that is there for the asking.

And this will be your story: one of beauty, a legacy in the memories of your precious ones, with visions of all the heroic moments of your life burned lovingly, skillfully, poignantly in the pathways of their hearts and minds, to be emulated in the future moments of their own.

Where is the victory over our storms, past, present, and future? It lies deep inside the potential of what each life can become. We bring the storms of our lives down to size because we know with full assurance that righteousness and redemption of each precious moment prevails, because He will prevail. And we will celebrate one another's stories for eternity, when we meet safely and securely one day with Him, in His glorious kingdom come.

An Anchoring
PRAYER

Heavenly Father,

My heart is beginning to slowly wrap around the idea that in this broken world, we will have trouble—just as Jesus told His disciples. I know the storms of loneliness, difficult seasons, disappointment, relational hurts, fear, and brokenness are always going to break upon my life because this is a broken world. God, help me settle that in my heart in a way that leads to acceptance and trust in you. You have promised to be always with me, to carry me through, to never leave me alone. Help me determine to live my life in such a way that those who watch me do so will be encouraged to also walk in faithfulness, hope, and grace. You are always so good to me, and you are the faithful Shepherd. Help me trust that in the midst of it all, I am held. In the precious name of Jesus, who loved me, and gave himself for me, Amen.

An Anchoring
SCRIPTURE

For no one can lay any foundation other than the one already laid, which is Jesus Christ. If anyone builds on this foundation using gold, silver, costly stones, wood, hay or straw, their work will be shown for what it is, because the Day will bring it to light. It will be revealed with fire, and the fire will test the quality of each person's work. If what has been built survives, the builder will receive a reward. If it is burned up, the builder will suffer loss but yet will be saved—even though only as one escaping through the flames.

1 CORINTHIANS 3:11–15 NIV

Christ is the foundation of our lives, the only way we can build something that will last. Take some time to consider the reality of His stability in your life. Think about your own building. Are you using gold, silver, and costly stones? Or wood, hay, and straw? What might it look like to change that? Keep in mind that while we want to build something that will last in order to leave an empowering example to others, it is truly the foundation that matters most of all.

An Anchoring
ACT

Imagine for a moment that you are able to look back at those you will one day leave behind. Write down what you think they might say about you. What sort of legacy are you leaving right now? How does your life show evidence of your receiving the grace and hope God offers to us in storms?

Now may the God of hope fill you with all joy and peace in believing, so that you will abound in hope by the power of the Holy Spirit.

ROMANS 15:13

STORM CARE KIT

1 Begin each day remembering and choosing to believe in the essential goodness of God's character.

> *Give thanks to the LORD, for He is good;*
> *For His mercy is everlasting.*
>
> PSALM 118:1

2 Understand and remember that Jesus warned us that this world is a broken place and will lead us through a pathway of storms and stresses.

> *These things I have spoken to you so that in Me you may have peace. In the world you have tribulation, but take courage; I have overcome the world.*
>
> JOHN 16:33

3 Remember that God understands your sadness, feelings, and lament in the midst of the storms.

> *The LORD is near to the brokenhearted*
> *And saves those who are crushed in spirit.*
>
> PSALM 34:18

4 Call on the Holy Spirit to give you wisdom, strength, and comfort.

> *But the Helper, the Holy Spirit whom the Father will send in My name, He will teach you all things, and remind you of all that I said to you.*
>
> JOHN 14:26

5 Arm yourself with beauty and gentleness. Let God take care of you.

> *Your right hand upholds me;*
> *And Your gentleness makes me great.*
>
> PSALM 18:35

6 Choose to trust God, to not allow your heart to be troubled when darkness overwhelms, and to live into the peace of Christ.

> *Peace I leave you, My peace I give you; not as the world gives, do I give to you. Do not let your hearts be troubled, nor fearful.*
>
> JOHN 14:27

Notes

Chapter 4 Broken Expectations

1. Sally Clarkson, *Dancing with My Heavenly Father* (Colorado Springs: Waterbrook, 2010), 75.

Chapter 5 Busyness + Distraction = Exhaustion

1. A. A. Milne, *House at Pooh Corner* (New York: Puffin Books, 1992), 169.

2. A. A. Milne, *Winnie-the-Pooh* (New York: Dutton Children's Books, 1988), 158.

Chapter 7 Disappointment in Marriage

1. "Prayer of St. Francis," Wikipedia, accessed February 10, 2021, https://en.wikipedia.org/wiki/Prayer_of_Saint_Francis.

Chapter 8 Unexpected Challenges with Our Children

1. Sally Clarkson and Nathan Clarkson, *Different: The Story of an Outside-the-Box Kid and the Mom Who Loved Him* (Carol Stream, IL: Tyndale Momentum, 2016), 1–2.

Chapter 11 Weathering a Lifetime of Storms Brings Character and Wisdom

1. James 1:13.

About the Author

Sally Clarkson is the bestselling author of more than twenty books, a world-renowned speaker, and a beloved figure who has dedicated her life to supporting and inspiring countless women to live into the story God has for them to tell. She delights in helping others live intimately within the abundant love of God.

Sally has been married to her husband, Clay, for almost forty years, and together they founded and run Whole Heart Ministries, an international ministry seeking to support families in raising faithful, healthy, and loving children in an increasingly difficult culture. Sally also encourages women through her LifewithSally.com membership community and Mom Heart Ministry small groups.

Sally and Clay have four children, Sarah, Joel, Nathan, and Joy, all writers in their own fields as academics, authors, actors, musicians, filmmakers, and speakers.

Sally lives between the mountains of Colorado and the rolling fields of England and can usually be found with a cup of tea in her hands. She loves the companionship of her family, thoughtful books, beautiful music, regular teatimes, candlelight, walking, and traveling to see her children.

SALLY CLARKSON

Author | Speaker | Lifegiver

Beloved author and speaker Sally Clarkson has dedicated her life to the art of mentoring women, encouraging mothers, and educating children. If you would like more daily encouragement in your life from Sally, visit her online at these websites and pages:

Website & Blog | **SallyClarkson.com**
Find daily encouragement for your journey as a woman, mom, and believer on Sally's blog as she shares thoughts, insights, inspiration, wisdom, recipes, traditions, and prayers. You can also stay up to date with her speaking schedule, events, and conferences.

Online Community | **LifewithSally.com**
Life with Sally is an online community of women that was created to reach, teach, and mentor moms worldwide in a more personal way. It is filled with Sally's talks, videos, recipes, Bible studies, workbooks, a forum, and more. It is an online resource to invite a bit of community, wisdom, and joy into today's women's worlds.

Podcast Page | **AtHomewithSally.com**
Sally invites you into her home and shares personal stories, spiritual insight, and hard-earned wisdom about being a woman, mom, and believer. Filled with dynamic and relevant guests, this podcast, which has been downloaded more than eight million times, will give you a personal and intimate connection into Sally's heart, mind, and home.

Social Media
Facebook | **@TheRealSallyClarkson**
Instagram | **@Sally.Clarkson**
Twitter | **Sally_Clarkson**

CLARKSON FAMILY BOOKS & RESOURCES

Sally Clarkson

- *Seasons of a Mother's Heart*
- *The Mission of Motherhood*
- *The Ministry of Motherhood*
- *Dancing with My Heavenly Father*
- *Desperate* (with Sarah Mae)
- *You Are Loved* (with Angela Perritt)
- *10 Gifts of Heart*
- *Your Mom Walk with God*
- *Own Your Life*
- *The Lifegiving Home* (with Sarah Clarkson)
- *The Lifegiving Table*
- *Different* (with Nathan Clarkson)
- *Only You Can Be You* (with Nathan Clarkson)
- *Girls' Club* (with Joy and Sarah Clarkson)
- *Mom Heart Moments*
- *Awaking Wonder*
- *The Awaking Wonder Experience* (with Clay Clarkson)

Clay Clarkson

- *Educating the WholeHearted Child, 4th ed.* (with Sally Clarkson)
- *Our 24 Family Ways*
- *Heartfelt Discipline*
- *Taking Motherhood to Hearts* (with Sally Clarkson)
- *The Lifegiving Parent* (with Sally Clarkson)

Sarah Clarkson

- *Journeys of Faithfulness*
- *Read for the Heart*
- *Caught Up in a Story*
- *Book Girl*

Nathan Clarkson

- *Good Man*

WHOLE HEART MINISTRIES

Keeping Faith in the Family

Whole Heart Ministries is a nonprofit Christian home and parenting ministry founded by Clay and Sally Clarkson in 1994. From the beginning, our mission has been to give help and hope to Christian parents to raise wholehearted children for Christ. Our current strategic ministry initiatives include Sally Clarkson Ministry, Mom Heart Ministry, Storyformed Project, Family Faith Project, Lifegiving Family Project, and WholeHearted Learning. We are keeping faith in the family.

Whole Heart Ministries
PO Box 3445 | Monument, CO 80132
719-488-4466 | 888-488-4466
whm@wholeheart.org | admin@wholeheart.org

For more information, visit our ministry website:
WholeHeart.org

Also from Sally Clarkson

In our outcome-based, technologically driven society, it is easy to lose sight of the innocence and uniqueness of each child. In these pages, Sally Clarkson helps parents unearth the hidden potential of their child's imagination, learning capacity, and ability to engage authentically with the world using the same principles that guided her in raising her four children.

Awaking Wonder

This companion guide to *Awaking Wonder* provides practical ideas, insights, and suggestions to direct you and your children along the path of wonder and learning. The *Awaking Wonder Experience* is a lifegiving map that will point you in the right direction by offering creative ideas, encouragement, and space to build your own twelve-month plan.

Awaking Wonder Experience

⟨ BETHANY HOUSE

 Stay up to date on your favorite books and authors with our free e-newsletters. Sign up today at bethanyhouse.com.

 facebook.com/BHPnonfiction

 @bethany_house

 @bethany_house_nonfiction